M000114340

THE GREAT INDOORSMAN

THE GREAT INDOORSMAN

Essays

Andrew Farkas

The University of Nebraska Press
Lincoln

© 2022 by the Board of Regents of the University of Nebraska
Acknowledgments for the use of copyrighted material appear
on pages 163–64, which constitute an extension of
the copyright page.
All rights reserved

Manufactured in the United States of America
The University of Nebraska Press is part of a land-grant
institution with campuses and programs on the past, present,
and future homelands of the Pawnee, Ponca, Oto-Missouria,
Omaha, Dakota, Lakota, Kaw, Cheyenne, and Arapaho
Peoples, as well as those of the relocated Ho-Chunk, Sac and
Fox, and Iowa Peoples.

∞

Library of Congress Cataloging-in-Publication Data
Names: Farkas, Andrew, author.
Title: The great indoorsman: essays / by Andrew Farkas.
Description: Lincoln: University of Nebraska Press, 2022.
Identifiers: LCCN 2021028955
ISBN 9781496230515 (paperback)
ISBN 9781496230935 (epub)
ISBN 9781496230942 (pdf)
Subjects: BISAC: BIOGRAPHY & AUTOBIOGRAPHY /
Personal Memoirs | HUMOR / Form / Essays |
LCGFT: Essays. | Autobiographies.
Classification: LCC PS3606.A694 G73 2022 |
DDC 814/.6 [B]—dc23
LC record available at https://lccn.loc.gov/2021028955

for Carl Peterson

CONTENTS

3   The Great Indoorsman

21   Wait Here?

27   A Filk Tale

39   Pool Hall Legend

45   Somewhere Better Than This Place

55   A Front or Affront

65   Kitchen Sink Realism

67   Time Stands Still When You're Havin' Fun

81   On Drinking the Kool-Aid in a Coffeehouse

87   Still Life with Alarm Clocks

103   Everything You Were Looking For

107   An Essay About Nothing

119   When Hamburger Station Is Busy

127   Last Year at Chapel Hill Mall

139   Bowl-a-Rama

143   Noir Girl

163   Acknowledgments

THE GREAT INDOORSMAN

The Great Indoorsman

Part the First

From A Philosophy of the Indoors – *The Sublime:* I often find myself in awe of the grandeur of the Indoors . . .

An excerpt from A Guide to the Indoors – *Weather:* "It's goddamned hot," said the old man.

Surrounding us were four walls that, for some time, weren't so much painted yellow, as they were yellowed; the folks who came up with the color, embarrassed, shame-filled, likely called it Cigarette Miasma to warn buyers, though Charlie, asleep in one of the booths, wasn't to be dissuaded, the price having been right—cheap.

"It's goddamned hot," the old man said.

Those four walls belonged to Kamper's, a dive bar in Munroe Falls, Ohio, the kind of place frequented by permanently surly old dudes who complain about how it's difficult to be a man in this shitty world, I mean you've gotta work hard all goddamned day, then you've gotta drink all fuckin' night, then you've gotta get the hell outta bed at the ass crack a dawn, head pounding pounding pounding, then you've gotta break your goddamned back for another ten, twelve hours (with a hangover like you wouldn't fuckin' believe), and after that, hell, there ain't no choice, what else ya gonna do to deal with all this bullshit, only one thing for a man to do, and that's go get yourself royally shitfaced, meaning Cigarette Miasma was definitely right for this joint, not the color it had suddenly become—pink. The price must've been right.

"It's goddamned hot," the old man said, adding: "And soon . . . it'll be winter. Then it'll be sonuvabitchin' cold! That's what it always is—goddamned hot or sonuvabitchin' cold."

If I were of age, I would've happily contributed to tomorrow's apparently mandatory hangover and bought him a beer. Since I wasn't, I chewed my cheeseburger and thought about the fact that in the summer we complain about the heat, about the humidity, or about the fact that it isn't as warm as we'd like; in the winter we complain about the cold, about the snow, about the ice; in the spring we complain that it isn't quite summer yet; in the fall we bemoan the coming of winter, and during all seasons we complain about rain. When the conversation lists toward the topic of weather, we stop actually conversing and engage in ancient, elaborate, and ritualized laments which ultimately remind us that our place in nature is not to be happy, that no matter where we are, something will *always* be wrong. Then I looked at those hideous pink walls, at those spots where the old sickly yellow oozed through, realizing it was only because of the air conditioning and because of those walls that we weren't being assaulted by the elements, that we weren't at the mercy of the weather.

The old man said: "But it's good to be in here."

And he was right. It was.

A fragment of The Indoorsiad, *or* The Epic of The Great Indoorsman – *The Origin Story:* See the petting zoo. Perhaps it's a barnyard, a grassy field, a slight hill (the paterfamilias unsure), the larger animals, possibly a cow, a llama, a zebra, a burro, a mini-horse, some hogs, all held back by gates with wide bars, all poking their snouts through the rungs, all waiting for pats on the head, all gleefully anticipating feed from ice cream cones, while roaming free are sheep, goats, little pigs, almost as free as the humans, the adult *Homo sapiens* corralling their unruly offspring, full of a boinging, inexhaustible energy, joyfully screaming, the parents enthusiastically directing their rollicking rug rats toward the more sedate creatures, the smaller creatures, so furry, so cute, everything designed to be almost unendurably adorable, when, encroaching upon this scene, came a stranger, shrouded in mystery by his vehicle, the stroller, pushed by he whom everyone assumed was the occupant's father, though the unlikely progenitor had dark, curly hair, dark eyes, dark skin (in short, a person made for the outdoors), while the inhabitant of the perambulator, as would later become apparent, had blonde, straight hair, green eyes, very pale skin (in short, a person made for a basement), toward this mismatched tandem, driven by some goat-instinct, probably stemming from his experience with previous tikes, a young Billy, having broken away from the other creatures, ambled, maybe with thoughts of food or nuzzling or whatever it is goats think about, and upon reaching his destination, Billy stuck his head into the pram.

As my father tells the story, retribution was quick: I, the young Indoorsman, without pause, clearly demarked Billy's proper space as being in the out-of-doors and my own space as being in the (in this case, makeshift) Indoors by instantaneously socking the goat in the nose, sending Billy staggering back, sending my dad into laughing hysterics, so shocked he would tell the story again and again throughout my life, "You gotta hear about the petting zoo . . ."

Now, whereas I write to you as The Great Indoorsman, I hope you will take three things into account when thinking about this anecdote: (1) as an adult, I do not sanction serving up knuckle sandwiches to goats at petting zoos, (2) as a very little child, I could not be expected to think rationally, and (3) since I was small enough to be in a stroller, the force of the blow was not exactly Kryptonian in magnitude.

That said, and with the emissary from the out-of-doors vanquished, I like to think, while my father recovered from his laughing fit, that the raucous atmosphere of the petting zoo went silent, the adults, the children, even the fauna turned in my direction as I laid back in my perambulator, the congregants recognizing not who I was, but who I would be, and when I gestured to my father, letting him know it was time to continue on, when he, once more, began propelling me forward, the denizens of the petting zoo looked on and, especially the beasts, as we passed, gave a very wide berth to The Great Indoorsman.

Part the Second

From A Philosophy of the Indoors – *Where I Lived, and What I Lived For:* I went to the Indoors because, like Henry David Thoreau, I *wished* to live deliberately, I *wished* to front only the essential facts of life and see if I could not learn what it had to teach, and not, when I came to die, discover that I had not lived, but . . . well, I found I wasn't exactly cut out for that sort of deal, see, it didn't really agree with me, so to speak, sounding rather Romantic and bombastic, like it'd take a heartier constitution than I have (the right hombre for the role being several orders of magnitude manlier than me), and require a whole lot more patience, the Spartan life leading to, like, watching ants fight it out and what have you, so I figured the unsucked marrow of life, sure, it'd be just fine encased in the bones of whatever larger being this metaphor is referring to, while in the meantime, I'd master resignation, not in a broken and defeated way, not in a fatalistic way, but more in the Falstaffian way of being gloriously resigned to the pleasures and experiences which suit me, those being the modulated wantonness and controlled chaos of the In-of-Doors, where we're not so concerned with reducing life to its lowest terms because that sounds like roughing it and, I mean, are you kidding me? not a chance, so, instead, here we let the burgeoning *human* world cut a fairly broad swath through our psyches (never shaving so close as to be intimidating, though), here we admire the Beautiful On-Purpose knowing it'll never drive us out of our comfort zones and into a corner, forcing us to act (as the out-of-doors most certainly would at some point), *and* here we finally put to rout the idea that there's something wrong with living inside, with its temperature control, and comfortable furniture, and lack of rampaging predators or slithering sacs of neurotoxin or airborne stinging pests, for most folks, it appears to me, think of the Indoors not as a habitat constructed lovingly for them, but as some sort of necessary evil that, truth be told, given our collective druthers (whoever stole them in the first damned place), we'd happily escape from, we'd "get away from it all," as they say, but, really, to where at would we go? I'm thinking it'd just be another space Indoors.

An excerpt from A Guide to the Indoors – *Shopping:* The Gallery Furniture cafeteria was almost empty. A ray of sunlight slanting through a gigantic window fell yellow on tables that needed busing, recently occupied by a horde of children and their spunky parents. It was a remarkably lonesome moment. Raucous music roared from the 450" telescreen.

Uncalled, a memory floated into my mind of a plush family room where me and my friends celebrate our New Year's Eve tradition, Bad Movie Night, everyone bringing one entertainingly lousy film, everyone joyously mocking. The trip to Gallery Furniture had been taken in the same vein, the store even mimicking one particular flick quite well: John Carpenter's *They Live* (1988), since pasted everywhere were slogans in black letters on white paper espousing capitalistic success via hard work and determination, espousing obnoxious forms of patriotism, espousing eye-rolling and groan-inducing Christian morality, but unlike in the film, these slogans were not subliminal, not hidden by alien technology, no, they were unabashedly on display, including, inexplicably, "What does not kill me makes me stronger," from Friedrich Nietzsche! Although completely out of place on the walls, Nietzsche would've fit in with us as we lampooned the Gallery Furniture coat of arms (which contained both a silhouette of the state of Texas and also the word "Texas" inside the silhouette to further establish the silhouette of Texas was indeed Texas and not some impostor state); the fact that this furniture store for some reason had shrines to Elvis and Princess Diana; the fact that this furniture store had a tennis machine with court and a medieval castle playground; the fact that it not only had a theatre marquee (Coming Soon! Chairs!) and a Vegas style sign, but was also as disorienting to walk through as any casino; the fact that the 450" TV obviously wasn't enough, so televisions were mounted absolutely everywhere, many of which were playing Gallery Furniture commercials inexorably demanding how delighted you'd be if you came to Gallery Furniture (no mention of what if you're already on site, begging the question: is there a higher plane Gallery Furniture? a mystical Gallery Furniture? is the vision of Gallery Furniture that I see your vision's greatest enemy?); the fact that cameras cover every square inch of this emporium, apparently fully embracing any dystopian vision you might have for the place; the fact that if you made a purchase, you received a red, white, and blue basketball completely covered with Gallery Furniture logos, so that you'd have an unimpeded view of that logo no matter how you held the ball; the fact that international flags pervaded, making us think Mattress Mack believes each of those countries is located in his store, which'd make sense, seeing as how his book, *Always Think Big*, might indicate the world's population will soon live under one banner: Gallery Furniture's; the fact that this wasn't really a furniture store at all, but a theme park dedicated to the outrageous, absurd, and insufferable spirit of this state, typified by Lone Star beer's ad slogan: "The *National* Beer of Texas" (italics mine).

But the lesson of Bad Movie Night is that whereas lampooning makes some of the films barely endurable, others come alive, and like their poorly constructed monsters, suck you inside, make you thankful they are the way they are, no matter how ludicrous, because you get to interact with them, you get to jeer at them, though your irony, your vitriol can never raise you above this travesty (so you can look down on it), can never truly get you outside of the thing itself.

But why would The Great Indoorsman want to be outside?

What has the outside ever done for him?

The Great Indoorsman gazed up at the gargantuan telescreen where Gallery Furniture owner Jim McIngvale was speaking rapidly, bopping and juking, about to leap from the two-dimensional world into the store. Forty minutes it had taken to understand the fuck?! I mean, really? Forty minutes. O cruel, needless misunderstanding! O stubborn, self-willed exile from the Texas-sized breast! Two Coca-Cola brand scented tears trickled down the sides of his nose. But it was all right, everything was all right, the struggle was finished. As the commercials relentlessly foretold, he was delighted, so extremely delighted, there are no small emotions here, intensely, terrifyingly delighted. Because he loved Gallery Furniture. And he knew Mattress Mack was going to save him money. TODAY!

A fragment of The Indoorsiad, *or* The Epic of The Great Indoorsman – *His Education:* Now the word of the Lord, or at least of St. Eugene's Church, came unto me, saying something along the lines of, "Arise, go to Mohican State Park, and commune with nature and your fellow adolescent parishioners, for your slothful wickedness brought on by the Nintendo and the television is repugnant to me." And although I was already well on the path to apostasy, a path my father had taken up long ago after being labeled a heretic by his grade school priest, after earning the report card assessment, NOT RECOMMENDED TO CONTINUE PAROCHIAL EDUCATION, and although I would've preferred to redirect this excursion to the waterslide park at Dover Lake, since exercise and sun and interaction with other teenagers could be obtained there, a place made of cement and plastic and metal and rubber and maybe like canvas and terrycloth, a place full of clean, chlorinated water, a place completely lacking in animals, a place not so mired in the out-of-doors, yes, in spite of all of this I chose to heed the call and go canoeing. Plus, I tried to convince myself, it'll be fun.

Fun.

And so, instead of fleeing into the basement as I should have, where *Dragon Warrior* and *Final Fantasy II* and *Simon's Quest* and *NHLPA Hockey* and other like entertainments awaited me, or alternatively where Australian Rules Football on ESPN and music videos on MTV and David Letterman reruns on A&E and other such diversions could be enjoyed, I went down to the end of my driveway and found there a minivan going to the general vicinity of Loud-onville, which is close to Mansfield (as the crow, omen of death, flies), Man-sfield itself a part of the vacuum that yawns between the Cleveland/Akron/ Canton area and the vast sprawl of Columbus, evidenced by the fact that our forebears chose to place a penitentiary in that, I guess, "city." Nobody lives there, so why not a prison?

Then, after a journey of six and eighty minutes, not one of which was spent by me thinking on the fact that I knew nothing about canoeing at all, that I'd never exhibited a single skill in anything outdoorsy, that I'd left the Cub Scouts with no plans whatsoever to join the Boy Scouts, we arrived at Mohican Ad-ventures, where we found boats aplenty for to deliver us to our ruin; so the adults paid the fare thereof, split us into crews of three, and launched us into the river. Have fun now!

There was that word again: fun.

Later, my education gave unto me a vision of Australia, where can be found, within or surrounding, all of the most venomous snakes and spiders and Muppet-like creatures (the platypus) and octopi and snails and Portuguese men-o-war (justifiably called "floating terrors") and fish and insects (be they innumerable) and jellyfish (some of which are immortal); so too can be found sharks (in unfathomable varieties) and crocodiles and dingoes and seemingly adorable creatures that, given but half a chance, will fuck you up (koalas and kangaroos). And though nary a one of these beasts hails from the State of the Buckeye (Ohio be praised!), they do exist, and in my vision I was beset by every last one of them, a caucus having been held, a covenant reached, wherein the aforementioned signees agreed to go about their busi-ness as per usual, unless given the unlikely opportunity to sting and to bite and to fill with neurotoxins and myotoxins and hemotoxins and nephrotox-ins The Great Indoorsman, and then to leave him alone so that he may expe-rience dizziness and convulsions and necrosis and fever and cardiac distress and larynx swelling and difficulty breathing and anxiety and severe headache and backache and nausea and vomiting and diarrhea and paralysis and the glorious impending doom brought on by Irukandji syndrome, and then to be slowly devoured, leisurely devoured while still somehow sensate, now, my fellow horrors, don't rush, enjoy yourselves, we've really been waiting for this, yes, should luck smile upon them, all of the terrifying monsters of the Land Down Under would work together in their ravagement of my person, but only once I reached an age when, it could be said, I should conceivably know better than to be anywhere near them. Thus their contract. But before the scales fell from my eyes, before my education was complete, I tried to convince myself, I tried to agree with the adults: this will be fun.

Fun it was not.

Part the Third

From A Philosophy of the Indoors – *The Beautiful On-Purpose and the Beautiful Accident:* The waitress looks at me and frowns. She says she's seen me before, thinks she's seen me before, is told that she has indeed seen me before. Baffled, befuddled, the waitress asks if I live in Chicago, says she lives in Chicago, says she's only here because it's a job, you know? but that she wouldn't be here if they weren't paying her, asks again if I live in Chicago, answers her own question, asks why . . . *why* do you come here?

The here she's referring to is the Signature Lounge on the 96th floor of the John Hancock Center. What I don't tell her is that we're two stories higher up than the observation deck. What I don't tell her is that the drinks may be overpriced where I currently sit, but that once I pay, I do end up with a drink, whereas my admission to downstairs only gets me an elevator ride and a view. What I don't tell her is that in this place I get the Beautiful On-Purpose, the Beautiful Accident, *and* the latter inside of the former, meaning even Chicagoans may find the journey to the Signature Lounge a long one, not because of the distance, since the CTA buses or trains and then the high-speed elevator will get you here lickety-split, but because the view is so beautiful that one is beguiled at every slight turn of the head, making the great golden seconds, minutes, hours go by uncounted, as you look down on the city, with its towering buildings of various architectures, with its roof-top swimming pools, with its glass and steel and cement and brick, a wholly human atmosphere, the reminder of which being the teeming and teaming hordes below, walking along the never-ending sidewalks, driving on the roads which stretch on forever through multitudinous neighborhoods, each with its own personality, as if the blocks themselves could turn into golems, could climb the exoskeleton of the John Hancock, could sit down next to you at the bar, could buy you a drink, ask you for a drink, threaten to smash a barstool across your teeth, offer to defend you, sell tickets to the fight, paint pictures of the bout, spin stories about mythical beings duking it out in the Signature Lounge over long forgotten slights, afterwards patrons swiveling slightly to gaze upon the other world, Lake Michigan, the sun reflecting off the blue, waves curling in, storms sending all of that fresh water into a white-capped tumult, the frigid winter crystalizing the lake, a transformation that reminds me of the religious language, the spiritual language outdoorsy types use to describe the wilderness, John Muir even seeing himself as a kind of prophet preaching the gospel of nature, of its vastness, of its sublimity, reminding me that Lake Michigan is nowhere near the largest body of water on earth, though it's much more than I can ever take in, that Lake Michigan is nowhere near the oldest body of water on earth, yet it's far older than me, will still be here when I'm gone, that all living creatures are pitted against this titanic assurance of death, and it is constantly our duty to break down any social customs, any norms, any systems that don't help us help each other, that don't bring us together as one people, such increasingly idyllic, idealized cerebrations being just the sort of thing modern day explorers seek when they get away from it all, though I'm having them Indoors, though I'm having them while admiring Lake Michigan from 960 feet up in the air through manmade glass windows that make it seem like I'm watching a movie so wonderfully shot, you'd swear it wasn't filmed thousands of miles from any urban center, it wasn't edited together nowhere near here, no, you'd swear it was taking place *right outside*.

Because it is.

I don't tell the waitress any of this.

Instead, I tell her I have friends in town.

She asks if they are of the invisible variety.

Instead, I say I wanted to see her again.

She doesn't buy that either.

Instead, I finish my drink and say I'll see her next week.

This . . . she believes.

An excerpt from A Guide to the Indoors – *Time:* In casinos, everyone knows what time it is. Sure, there are the conspiracy theories, about the carpet with the loud, disorienting patterns; about the reverberating din dominating the aural landscape; about the labyrinthine paths that somehow never lead to your destination; about the reason those pit bosses are so happy to give you free alcohol; about that extra oxygen they pump in (oh, everyone loves the oxygen, everyone loves the pumping, maybe the only known example of air porn,

"You know, hyuck hyuck, what they do, they pump, boy do they pump! they pump that oxygen right on in here, they do, oh yeah they do!"); about the diabolical interior designers who, satanically inspired, nixed windows from blueprints so their cave-like creations would obfuscate the natural world from patrons, would make you forget that the sun rises, that the sun sets, that the world continues on outside; *and* there are the conspiracy theories about the vilest casino ploy, the great granddaddy of them all—the fact that there are no clocks, no clocks anywhere, not a single one, and you can be certain that all of these ingenious, insidious, and most importantly *secret* schemes are operating because every last person in a casino will tell you about them. That's why, in the days before smartphones, with their satellite connections, with their links to atomic chronometers, those of the Indoors wore watches as a "fuck you" to the unseen security force, as a pointed "Save that shit for the tourists" to the nefarious powers-that-be, proving a sucker may be born every minute, but we Indoorsmen came screaming into the world knowing there's no evidence P.T. Barnum ever spoke those words.

But if we're all too aware that gambling dens use nefarious gambits to trick us, to coerce us into staying, why don't we avoid them? Because part of the casino experience is knowing why the carpet's so hideous, is knowing how to block out that din, is knowing the maze will get you there . . . eventually, is knowing why our drinks are free (and not particularly caring), is knowing why the air is of such high quality, is knowing why we can't see the outdoors (and not particularly missing it), is knowing enough to wear a watch, and, most importantly, is knowing that the casino has taken the time to construct ploys that entertain us while we're waiting for the next spin of the wheel, the next hand, the next dice roll, and has even made those schemes simultaneously believable (oh, we do love our secret knowledge) and transparent (doesn't this bastard realize a building full of pure oxygen would explode?!). The conspiracies are so powerful *because* they don't actually exist. The gamblers and the casinos therefore live in symbiosis: we know; they know we know; we know they know we know; there's nothing to know; everyone's happy.

Outside, there are storms in the middle of the day that can blacken the sky, in the fall and winter daylight savings confuses us, as do the late sunsets of summer, and during any season the weather can turn unseasonable forcing you to wonder just when any of this is happening. But here, Indoors, thanks to the casino's conspiracies, thanks to the Indoorsmen cracking their conspiracies, thanks to this fiction both sides accept, we *always* know *exactly* what time it is.

A fragment of The Indoorsiad, *or* The Epic of The Great Indoorsman – *The Journey:* Behold, in medias res, the inauspicious beginning to our adventure, for just beyond the first bend in the Mohican River, the Lord sent out a great current, nay, so the ghost of Dick Frye (founding father of canoeing in Ohio) sent out a great current, nay, so perhaps just the stream sent out a great current, rifling our boat and us in it toward the riverbank where grew a tree diagonally over the water. Then, with me at the back, in quick succession, each canoeist became exceedingly afraid for his head, and cried out profanities to no one in particular, and made the decision to whirl to the right, which was away from the wooden fiend, thus capsizing the vessel and casting us forth into the river, as if this were a set piece in a film by Buster Keaton, praise his name!

And, lo, the slapstick hijinks were not at an end, for before the three of us could regain our bearings, we capsized the boat times innumerable whilst attempting to get back on board, which didn't quite lead to my crewmates seeking the reason, randomly casting lots even, for whose cause this not quite evil, more like bad luck was upon us, but in hindsight it should have. I mean, come on. Seriously.

Nevertheless, the canoe was finally righted, the crew aboard (at last!) and rowing, which propelled the boat through the water of the Mohican, easily skimming along, so easily that we spoke out with great mirth, everyone to his fellow, about the oddity and, we prophesized (incorrectly), singularity of our misadventure, believing the rest of the day would be spent taking in the various trees and plants with their specific types of leaves and their colors, all of which flora assumedly having names, or, at least, would soon have names bestowed upon them when the name-givers came to realize this vegetation was anonymous; and wouldn't that be nice, knowing the true identities of more things that stuck in the ground in the forest, a thought that warmed my wet corpse as we continued gliding, now slowly, now more quickly, now coming to a screaming halt as if the canoe had brakes similar to those on an automobile. For *that* is what happened. Like, really.

And it was so, when we realized the river moved on, though we stood stockstill, that we began to doubt our senses, that we began to construct curious belief systems (each to his own), that we began and quickly aborted many explanatory speeches, likely convincing onlookers, should there have been any, that we'd been granted the gift of tongues. Wha um now gah say yeah uh, were the words we used. Wha um now gah say yeah uh, came the refrain.

After this time of great ignorance, we did learn that the out-of-doors had prepared a tree (another tree) that sprouted forth from the riverbed, or, contrarily, that the out-of-doors had prepared for that tree to grow and flourish and then fall into the river to impede our progress; no matter which, this second wooden fiend now lay just below the surface, two of its limbs forming a perfect canoe pincer-trap, curse the murkiness of unchlorinated water forever and ever! And so, we began rocking back and forth harder and harder to wrench ourselves away from the branches, ceasing only when we recalled our previous misadventure. Then, we tried using the oars as levers, thinking we could pry ourselves from nature's cruel grip, to no avail. The river flowed and flowed, though we went nowhere. Finally, enraged, we rained great blows down upon our captor with the paddles, with our hands, with anything available, until we were, of course, pitched into the river and our boat, free at last! spun and sank to the bottom.

Now, did my crewmates say unto me, as we hauled the canoe up from under the water, Tell us, goddamnit, for whose cause this bad luck is upon us; what the hell do you do? Whence do you come from? Like, what country are you even from? And, for fuck's sake, what people spawned you?

If they had, I would've responded, saying, I am an Indoorsman, and I fear I've come to where I do not belong, maybe, I dunno, accidentally, or hopefully, or something. But don't worry, because after this I ain't never coming back. Like, for real.

But they did not ask.

They and I with them remained silent, possibly picturing the activity of canoeing, each in our own minds, as one that involved the boat corkscrewing down any given river, regularly flinging its passengers into the water, a description I later relayed to my mother, who thence proclaimed that she would not be joining me should there be any future trips downstream.

Of course, her speech was superfluous, for there were none.

Now, were we able to right the boat, to bail out the water, to get back on board, to continue down the river? We were able. But I knew what would happen soon enough, saying as much unto my crewmates, unto the unnamed flora, unto the alien fauna, "We're gonna end up in the river again before this is over"; thus my prophecy. Did we end up in the river again? We did. We most certainly did.

But my newfound gift for seeing the banal hereafter failed to lighten the mood.

And so, it came to pass that we reached Frye's Landing much later than the rest of the group, a group including the very young and the very old, the ringing stories of unimpeded joy from the others supplying not the least bit of comfort, the mirth my crewmates and I exhibited earlier conspicuously absent since dripping was the only sound we gave off as we waited for it all to end. Then, not a moment too soon (perhaps, even, many moments too late), the minivan came and swallowed me up, transported me from Central to Northeast Ohio, and finally spat me out in the suburbs of Akron. In my mind, I heard the voice again, saying, "Arise, go to Mohican State Park, and commune with nature and your fellow adolescent parishioners, for your slothful wickedness brought on by the Nintendo and the television is repugnant to me," and realized the correct answer was, "No." Damp still, I left the out-of-doors, I left the outside, I threw open the screen that was all that stood between me and sanctuary, and at last entered my house. Though only a day had passed, it felt like many. But now I was Indoors.

I was home.

Part the Last

From A Philosophy of the Indoors – *The Out-of-Doors vs. Outside:* In Lawrence, Kansas, a Lyft driver asks me where my accent's from, says she's lived lots of places, says she has a good ear for accents, says that I do a good job of covering it up, but that I definitely have one, says if I give her a moment she'll tell me where I'm from. Since uncertainty is rampant in our lives and always has been, this opportunity might sound exciting, what with a stranger appearing who can teach me about myself, what with a stranger appearing who can dispel a bit of chaos from my world, but I already know what she's going to say, I even know her mental processes. The answer came to her immediately. The problem—something seemed off. Oh, the word that described my accent was right there, probably glowing before her very eyes, tracer lights racing around the cursive letters, the absolutely undeniable reply, but, for reasons unknown, she feared it. It just didn't seem right . . .

Her confusion may be yours too, there in the future, after you approach me, after you argue that I must've left the In-of-Doors at some point, after you say I must've enjoyed myself outside even if it was only once. It's true, you can't spend your entire life Indoors (no matter how hard you try). And it's true, I *have* enjoyed myself outside. But just as you think you've won, just as you think you've exposed me as a fraud (like learning Thoreau made side treks into town during his Walden Pond years), I will put you in the same state of mind as my Lyft driver by saying, "But, you see, the outside is *not* the out-of-doors."

There she is, the Lyft driver, looking at the glowing letters that make up the word that describes my accent, refusing to believe she'll say that ridiculous word, knowing that she'll absolutely say it.

There you are, looking at my baffling sentence, refusing to accept the fact that *outside* and *out-of-doors* are anything but synonyms, while simultaneously knowing they aren't synonyms at all.

Never fear, it isn't my goal to increase the amount of confusion in the world, so allow me to elaborate. First, I'll leave the Lyft driver in suspense no longer, I'll allow her to say what she's going to say, no matter how odd it may seem, an answer that's in full agreement with a Walgreen's cashier in Billings, Montana, and with a guy named Manny who I run into at Harbour Lights, a bar in Lawrence: Europe. You got it, all three of them tell me I have a European accent. Manny even adds, "Yeah, that's right. You have a European accent. I know, yeah, that's not a thing. European accent, sure, that's not a thing. But . . . you have one."

Now, since Europe is made up of fifty countries, many of which speak their own languages, different sections of which speak their own dialects, you might agree with an old colleague of mine who says that anyone who guesses "European" doesn't have a good ear for accents. But I disagree. Hence, I will use the division between the *outside* and the *out-of-doors* to explain myself, and to do so allow me to call your attention to St. Petersburg, Russia. When I was there, I found it strange that I couldn't tell the difference between the rivers and the canals. It wasn't because they both looked like rivers; it was because they both looked manmade. Lined with perfectly cut granite and guard rails, if the water were chlorinated and littered with inner-tubes, the city could've been a vast waterslide park, many of which are outside, none of which are in the out-of-doors. As Hercule Poirot says in *The Mysterious Affair at Styles*, "Have you ever been to New York, Hastings? [. . .] It is a beautiful city. Beautiful. There each street is at right angles to each avenue and each avenue is numbered nicely, First, Second, Third, Fourth. Man is in command there. But here, how does one live with the fact that [...] nature is untidy, uncontrolled, anarchic, inefficient?" St. Petersburg has merely extended this order to the very waterways. Consequently, the outside exists in the same place as the European accent—both of them are vast liminal spaces defined by what they aren't, rather than what they are, including the liminal space between existent and non-existent.

And so, when I say that I have enjoyed the outside before, will enjoy the outside again in the future, you shouldn't be concerned. Instead, you should find yourself at ease because the next time you throw open your door, step over the threshold, leave the comfort of the In-of-Doors, you won't be plagued with doubt, wracked with uncertainty because you will have heard the explanation of The Great Indoorsman, and thanks to the (questionable, even suspicious) authority granted him by his (mysterious and, come on, non-existent) European accent, you will know *exactly* where you are.

An excerpt from A Guide to the Indoors – *Where to Stay:* Up on the second floor of a Wellsburg, West Virginia, apartment building that doesn't offer a view of Charles Street, nor its row of questionable factories or warehouses, but instead overlooks a kind of backyard made up of broken glass, busted cement, cigarette butts, random trash, and a garden of assorted unsightly plants that could be called weeds, except they're certainly the most attractive inhabitants of that land, well up above is a one bedroom flat with smudged and beat-to-hell walls, one bearing a handwritten sign which reads: "I have gone in search of breakfast. If I never return, I expect there will be a week of mourning." And, should you go for a visit, should you check in to this magnificent wreck, you too can live like a Bohemian. For your convenience, the apartment is heated by a wall-mounted electrical element that, surprisingly, will not set the place ablaze someday, will never set the place ablaze, but will confer upon you fiery visions of imminent conflagrations, perfect imagery for later poems or stories written in a Beat style that you'll abandon before you ever finish them; the roof has collapsed in the unit across the hall, luckily while your neighbor (whom you've never seen, but you *have* consistently heard banging around as if he couldn't find the escape hatch into the world) was out, giving you the added benefit of wondering if your own ceiling might come tumbling down soon (now? okay, now, certainly now); the shower doesn't work, so you have to take a bath for the first time since childhood, so you have to think about the fact that, by the end, you're actually, although briefly, wallowing in your own filth; the toilet doesn't work either, so you have to piss in the sink, so you have to become friends with the people who work at the deli down the street when you have to shit, though luckily said employees are more than happy to ignore anyone who comes in; the woman next door howls all night long, screaming at no one, raging about nothing real either because she's an addict or because she's crazy or because she's been hired to act like an addict, to act crazy in order to inspire you to revisit your ill-conceived Beat writings; the windows don't quite seal, so the roving band of Houdini cats will eat the donuts you found when you ventured forth and then left on the coffee table, will escape before you can ever catch them, before you ever actually know it's them, what roving band of cats? I've never seen any cats, they're right behind me, up! must've escaped again cuz I didn't see anything; the lights in the stairwell and the hallway burned out so long ago no one's sure if it's the bulbs or the wiring or if the ancient ones who built this heap didn't bother with illumination, meaning when you return late at night, you have to slink up the steep stairs (sometimes on all fours), then drag your hand down the wall, counting the doors, now was it four or five, did I count four or five, do I live at four or five, oh, the screaming lady, so it's the next one. But there's more.

If you have time for the extended package, you can enjoy the deteriorating interior, the inept maintenance man whose idea of fixing your commode is giving you the parts (some of them even for a toilet) and shrugging his shoulders, saying, "I figure you got this"; you can enjoy the panic that comes on when you realize you forgot to pay the rent one month; you can further enjoy the ironic detachment that comes on when this lack of payment continues for half a year with no repercussions; you can see what it's like to eat food stolen from the grocery store after you lose your job; you can yawn at the unsurprising theft of your own personal property; you can marvel at the arrival of the police and the press (there's a newspaper!), and the arrival of the obviously mobbed-up landlord who shouts, "Goddamn it! You owe me two months' rent!" (which is hilarious because you owe him six months' rent). All of this and more is waiting for you Indoors!

Now, if you don't have time for the extended package, but still want the experience, you can opt for the long-distance service that will kick in after your brief visit, and subsequently you'll be called at 3:00 a.m. and via

stream-of-consciousness phone conversations you'll get the Bohemian existence vicariously, so later in life you'll have the parts you actually witnessed
and the ones you were told about, the two fusing together in the fiery confla-
gration (that only exists in your mind) brought on by the heating element,
burning the smudged and beat-to-hell walls, burning the ruinous (but surprisingly comfortable) couch, burning the treacherous staircase, burning the
collapsing roof, burning the extending and contracting hallway (was it four
or five or maybe even three?), the last thing to go being a sign, possibly mis-
remembered, that says: "I have gone in search of breakfast. If I never return, I
expect there will be a week of mourning."

I, myself, haven't returned to the Charles Street apartment for many years.
And whereas I have no evidence either way, I believe, I mean truly believe, upon
my disappearance the week of mourning was not only observed, but is observed
still, every year, on the anniversary of the last visit of The Great Indoorsman.

A fragment of The Indoorsiad, *or* The Epic of The Great Indoorsman – *The
Prophecy of The Great Indoorsman:* In the future, at some point, you'll ask me
to go camping with you. Do not despair: it has happened before, it will happen
again. When you do, when you extend to me this invitation, I will be polite,
I will listen to your pitch, I will encourage you to relive your favorite memories of bucolic surroundings, of life in the out-of-doors. Ultimately, you'll
talk about getting away (as if there were anything to escape), about returning
to our roots (though I was born inside), about the majesty of various mountains, about the terrifying sublimity of the jungle, about the serenity of the
forest, about the brutal beauty of the desert, about the ponderous expanse of
the plains, about pristine lakes, about vast oceans, about rolling rivers, about
nature. In a compromise, you'll perhaps even offer the rambunctious joy of
mainstream campsites, where each lot has electrical outlets, where shower
houses and bathrooms are to be found, where stores and even restaurants are
nearby, where carousers sit around fires, underneath the stars, drink beer from
the can, and soak *it* all in . . .

Definition of it *and explanation as to why* it *must be absorbed:* Unspecified,
likely unspecifiable.

. . . When I appear impassive, stoical, you will say, with maximum confusion, with maximum frustration, "For goodness sakes! It's the outdoors!"

From the comfort of a temperature-controlled room, I will inform you that I have been . . . to the out-of-doors. It's . . . it's not for me.

Dazed, despondent, defeated, you'll depart headed in the direction of whatever sort of nature you prefer. Will that be the end? It will not. For while you are hemmed in by that flora, while you are surrounded by that fauna, you'll get an idea. . .

Nature of the idea: Epiphanic, delusional.

. . . "If only," you will think, "I could formulate the right words, the proper phrases, the precise sentences, then I could convince His Indoorsiness to venture forth into nature."

Will you succeed this time? The only reason I'm able to bring myself to tell you that you will not is because you won't believe me. For, upon returning from your expedition, you'll be rejuvenated, restored, revitalized, you will have been made whole by the open air, so when you step foot back into civilization, you won't do so as a bowed and broken subject of the modern world, but as an explorer, a conqueror, the one being who can bend the will of anyone, no matter how resolute. And so, completely confident, absolutely assured, replete with resolve, in the name of nature, you will go forth and seek out the lair of The Great Indoorsman.

You'll know where to find me.

for Maria Ortiz

Wait Here?

Why do you hate the waiting room?

Because of the way it looks? What's it like? Do you remember? If pressed, could you rattle off, say, your five favorite waiting rooms with a list of their primary, secondary, tertiary, and quaternary features? Then, would it be possible for you to throw in the dates and times you visited them? You think there aren't detectives who can check up on these things? You think they haven't *already* checked up and we're now interested in seeing if you decide to lie? But, seriously, does a waiting room ever stick with you? If you left this waiting room right now, walked around the block, and returned, would you be able to state with certainty that it was the same waiting room? If it were different, would you notice? If it were the same, is there a chance you might think it was different? Have you, in the end, either consciously or unconsciously, accepted the fact that there's a template in your mind labeled Waiting Room, and that's all you've got no matter how disparate the places might actually be? Does it bother you that somehow a number of your experiences have taken place in an unidentifiable void? Or, without thinking about it, do you just sit there, surrounded by who knows what, and, innocuous activities notwithstanding, do you just sit there and *wait*?

Is the waiting room uncomfortable?

The furniture, does it appear to be from a boardroom, a convention center, a church basement, a college classroom, a dorm, a high school, a kindergarten, or maybe somebody's home? If it's like parlor furniture, what kind of parlor? Are you getting the brandy, cigars, and a whole lot of harrumphing vibe? The little sandwiches, Easter colors, and passive aggression vibe?

Or, are you thinking more like a fraternity house vibe, bunch of mismatched couches, wrecked chairs, tables that look like they were heaved off the roof and somehow landed here? Maybe there's an island theme, a nautical theme, a modernist theme, an antique theme, a 1950s theme, a far-flung future floating through space theme, or maybe the theme is that there's no goddamn theme at all? Would it be worse if there were no theme because you might begin to lose the thread of why you're here? Are you sweating through your pants onto this relentlessly unthemed furniture on account of whatever lies beyond this room waiting for you? Could it be that bad? Mightn't it be good? Or, is it possible that nothing's waiting for you? Does that calm you down or make you more apprehensive? Can you imagine, after you've heard your name called, standing up from your La-Z-Boy, walking through the door, down a hallway, then another, and finally being shown into the office where, as it turns out, there's nothing? How would nothing be represented? If you can't imagine any of that happening, but it did happen, would you shiver with fear and confusion, fondly remembering the halcyon times back in the coziness of the waiting room, when you sat in a club chair/wingback chair/wobbly folding chair/1950s desk-for-second-graders chair basking in the glow of your purpose, your absolutely real, even verifiable purpose for being there? If commanded to rank the three potential outcomes, would you list them Good—first, Bad—second, Nothing—447th? Would you gladly eliminate Good if you could also eliminate Nothing? Are you afraid when you *are* called, that you might stick to your chair? Or, maybe you don't worry at all, confident in your appointment, perched atop your comically short stool, and question instead, rightly so perhaps, whether a fraternity house, no matter how it's designed, could ever contain a room justifiably called a "parlor"?

What's the décor like in the waiting room?

Is there any art on the walls? If there is, and you originally saw this art at a friend's place, would you think less of that person? If you originally saw this art at a friend's place and recalled enjoying it, would you think less of yourself? If you originally saw this art at the store, purchased it, brought it home, hung it in a prominent place so everyone could gaze upon what you'd bought, no, what you'd finally obtained, acquired, added to the collection even, would you think, there in the waiting room, "Whelp, that's all for me," while rolling up your sleeves and producing the packet of razorblades you've kept at the ready for just such an occasion? Really, though, who produces this art? A student looking for a paycheck? A hack who's making a mint? A sad-sack who's lost all hope of realizing their dreams, or someone who never had any? A computer? How likely are you to accept "spontaneous generation" as a good explanation for the presence of this what-have-you? If we could go back in time to before the previous question was asked, are you thinking you'd never have answered "spontaneous generation," but now that the toothpaste is out of the tube (as it were), do you find it impossible to gin up any other plausible account for this . . . will we be sticking with *art*? After all, it's inconceivable that someone, anyone, an artist (no less), sat down, tools at the ready, ideas skittering through their mind, work progressing, progressing, moments of doubt, no, no, I can't do it, I'll *never* finish, but, must go on, yes, yes, at last! now take this, immediately, not there, no, not there either, no, take this *directly* to the dentist's office and put it in the waiting room—that's just a preposterous explanation, right? So, we're sticking with spontaneous generation? Do you imagine how your decision would be depicted on the walls of this waiting room?

Is there anything to do in the waiting room?

How about magazines? Does it seem, and maybe this is crazy talk, like magazines, the kind that sit in waiting rooms, stopped being produced say twenty, twenty-five years ago? When you see there are magazines, do you immediately check if they're from the last century? If they aren't, do you marvel at their existence? Do you imagine a cynical publisher that reprints magazine covers where the only thing that's changed is the date? Are you of the belief you'd actually notice? Will you later recall that you spent part of the day reading an honest to goodness magazine? What are the chances that something you read will actually be important, like really important, the sort of insight with the power to change everything if you actually followed it? Buried amongst so much garbage, though, will you realize how essential this insight is? Or, later, will you only think, "Now what was that I read today?" Will you dismiss it? Or will you grow frantic, race back to the waiting room, tear through the magazines? Do any of them have names you recognize, or are all of them suspiciously similar to names you think used to belong to magazines, but these, no way? Will you imagine a writer, ensconced in an impossibly gigantic building, who wrote that line for you and you alone? If you do, what was their endgame? Did they insanely believe you'd come along, see the sentence, and make the appropriate change before continuing on with the usual nonsense? Is it your opinion that this has been the problem thus far, that you just haven't stumbled upon the right magazine? Do you think it's being kept from you? Who's to blame? Would you actually use the word "thus" in any situation? Are you perhaps of the opinion that no person is to blame, but more like an entity? What is it? Where is it? Can it be found? Can it be stopped? Is it already too late? Is your belief in this entity your darkest secret? Who will reveal your shame? Which magazine you think it'll be in? Has the issue come out already? Do they have it here in the waiting room?

Does anyone work in the waiting room?

Can administrative assistants or receptionists or front desk people or secretaries be said to work in waiting rooms? Would your answer be the same if you knew they weren't waiting for anything? Is it possible to not be waiting for something? Were you waiting for me to ask that question? But, seriously, if they're not waiting, can they be in a *waiting* room? If not, where are they? How is it that you can see them? Do you remember talking to them? Do you remember their names? Would you say they looked like you (though not specifically you, but more the species you happen to belong to), or would you say they looked like a close facsimile of you (your species)? How close? Flawless, meaning you're certain they're *Homo sapiens*? Suspicious, meaning you're not certain, meaning there's an Uncanny Valley effect going on here? Close Enough, meaning . . . can you imagine someone answering "Close Enough"? Is it possible there are more "Close Enough" answerers than we originally thought . . . possible? Do you think I used the word "possible" twice in the past sentence because I'm lazy, or because I'm gobsmacked to realize there might not only be people who, when confronted with a potential *Homo sapiens* impostor, would say, "Meh, close enough," and then go on about their business as the counterfeit humans proceeded with the next phase of their impenetrable scheme, but that there might be a great many of these so-called Close Enoughs? Do you find yourself furtively inspecting the other folks around you to see if *they* are mimics, or the real deal? Or, would you rather pretend that everyone here is in the same room you're in, meaning they're all human, meaning they're all waiting? Then for what, exactly? When will its terrifying provenance come to pass? Or maybe, when will its glorious genesis be visited upon the world? Or, more likely, when will this banal bullshit go down?

Are all rooms waiting rooms?

How come they haven't called your name yet? Isn't it time for your appointment? Isn't it time to prove you have a purpose for being here? You *do* have a purpose for being here, right? Have you ever sat in a waiting room for so long, you forgot what you were waiting for? If so, did you come back to your senses? If you came back to your senses, how'd you explain the experience to yourself? Did you just end up assuming something happened behind the scenes that you'd never become privy to? Does anything ever happen in a waiting room? If it did, could that room still be called a waiting room? Is that why you hate being here, because you have more important things to do? Be honest—do you have more important things to do? Do you have *anything* to do? If you were liberated from this place, where would you go? Would you have fun? Would you be productive? Or, would you return home, sit down, stare into the middle distance, maybe occasionally flipping through, say, an honest to goodness magazine? Would you wonder what theme your furniture follows (if any)? Would you speculate about the art on the walls? Would you suddenly find yourself suspicious of the people there, the *others*? Do you now look at the waiting room, including everything and everyone in it, as a purposefully flimsy façade that mocks your normal, everyday existence? Do you feel yourself becoming part of the waiting room? Are you still of the belief that your name will be called? Have you come to the conclusion that you're exactly where you're supposed to be? Or, on the other hand, if you *have* waited so long you forgot what you were waiting for, is there a chance you *never* returned to your senses? Maybe that's why you're here, to get your life back, the life you lost in a waiting room? Then how come they didn't usher you directly to the person you're here to see? Does it make any sense that you were guided, likely by someone with an unnerving smile, into this godawful place after what happened to you? Are you back to wondering what you're doing here now? But, then, they're not holding you against your will, are they? Couldn't you just go? Is there anything or anyone stopping you from standing up, walking across the lobby, throwing open the door, and confidently striding right into whatever is to come? Why can't you do that? Wouldn't it be better than rotting away in here? Will it really be that great when your name is finally called? Or, at this stage, do you expect something transcendent will happen? You know it's not going to, though, right? And yet, you're still sitting here? Why?

I mean seriously, what are you waiting for?

A Filk Tale

If you knew the words, as I stood there on the porch outside my rundown duplex cottage in Tuscaloosa, Alabama, holding in one hand a torn envelope with no return address on it, the other hand a Days Inn business card bearing the inscription, "IT'S WHERE I WANT TO BE!!! —JIM," sun beating down on me, same sun that beat down on Carthage when it was such a threat to Rome that Cato the Elder decided, no matter what he was originally bloviating about, to end every last one of his speeches to the senate with, "And I believe Carthage must be destroyed," which prompted me and the writer of the inscription to conclude our elaborate and ridiculous emails to each other with that same line, well, if you knew the words you could join me, wherever you are in space and time, you could join me, or that younger version of me, you could join me . . . because as soon as I read Jim's note, I began to sing . . .

When Bill Taylor wrote the lyrics to "Benson, Arizona," in 1973, he thought he'd invented the country-and-western science fiction song. But actually, *filk* music, being a combination of folk and the science fiction, fantasy, and/or horror genres, had been around since the 1950s. The prehistory of filk, however, extends back even further. In 1937, after a schism in the Greater New York Science Fiction Club, a new group of SF aficionados formed: The Futurians. Originally, The Futurians were just fans of science fiction, though later many of them would become writers and editors (Isaac Asimov, for instance). Two members who would become authors, Frederik Pohl and Cyril Kornbluth, also penned protest songs that used tropes from their preferred genre. These tunes, which at the time had no specific classification, would inspire and influence the music that's now called filk.

Me and Jim Westlake hadn't heard of filk at the time. What we'd heard of, we'd heard of a movie about space explorers whose only job was to destroy planets with irregular orbits, so those planets couldn't (potentially) smash into local stars and (possibly) devastate future (theoretical) human colonies; we'd heard of a film that featured sentient, egotistical bombs that threatened the lives of the astronauts; we'd heard the opening credits were backed by a country-and-western song influenced by Einstein's relativity and interstellar travel; we'd heard there was a sequence in this flick that was supposed to take place in an elevator shaft, but which was obviously shot in a hallway; we'd heard there was an alien on board the title ship that was definitely a beach ball with rubber claws; we'd heard it was Dan O'Bannon's first movie (the *Alien* screenwriter); we'd heard it was John Carpenter's first movie (the director of *Halloween* and *Escape from New York*). We'd heard of *Dark Star* (1974). But even though we looked and looked, we weren't able to find a copy of it.

Until we learned of Ozoner Video.

Now, back in the '90s, if you lived in Columbus, Ohio, and you wanted a cult film, did you go to Ozoner Video? If you wanted a flick full of bad acting and questionable special effects, did you go to the industrial part of town? If you wanted something obscure, something that made you wonder how in *the* hell this movie ever got made, did your car lead you to some building looked like maybe it'd been abandoned a good decade ago?

Hell, no.

Instead, what you did, you went to North Campus Video, being right next to, you know? the Ohio State campus, up on North High Street. Had a bright blue awning. Couldn't possibly miss the place. And there, on well-organized and categorized shelves, you'd probably find the cinematic oddity you wanted—flicks like *Chicken Boy* (being the exploits of a character who is "One part chicken, the other part boy") or *Radioactive Dreams* ("Just your typical action-adventure-science fiction-musical-fantasy in the post-nuclear world" kind of movie). And if you had trouble locating what you were look-ing for, Magneto (because we'd never seen anyone before or since with more piercings), well, Magneto, with his permanent scowl, would find it for you. Would he finally smile when you complimented him for knowing every bi-zarre movie in the world, when you thanked him for pinpointing . . . ?

Hell, no.

But he would growl, "No problem," running his hand over his bald head, and you'd feel good knowing he was there, knowing that this *institution* existed, this place that contained every film, no matter how arcane. Even if you didn't live in Columbus. Even if you only saw him once a semester . . .

Maybe that's what happened. Maybe Magneto (our guide through the cinematic backwater, our hierophant) knew when people had grown too dependent on him, knew when it was time to cast his followers out into the world to have their own adventures. So, when he sees you, having combed through North Campus Video again, but *what the hell?* found nothing, he knows you're gonna come, bowing, reverent, asking, pleading for guidance from your guru once more, only this time there won't be any. Instead, and Magneto's done it all before, there *will* be (feigned) shock. Could be he'll even throw in *awestruck*, saying, "No . . . I've been looking to get a copy of *Dark Star*, but I haven't been able to find it."

And so, that's when our quest began.

. . . who knows, maybe, across space, you're joining Jameses II and Andysseus (as we called ourselves in emails wherein we plotted against each other, against rival schools, against the world, the galaxy, the universe even), who knows, maybe you are joining us across time, following that bouncing ball in your mind, because, to be honest, although alone on that porch, I didn't feel like I was singing a solo, or even a duet, nah, felt I'd entered a bit late, the crowd already chiming in, having taken their cue from the front man, who of course had shouted, "Now everybody—," didn't matter that no one was around but yours truly, much as it didn't matter to Cicero that he'd never met Cato the Elder, never met anyone who had, Cicero just knew in his heart how the old man finished his speeches, yeah, sure, there on the porch, the lead singer, the guitar picker, the bassist, the drummer, the fans themselves may've been corporeally absent, but that didn't stop them, didn't stop me, so it shouldn't stop you from belting out the words, since you're now a member of this here ethereal band . . .

Filk itself didn't really get going until science fiction conventions got big. They didn't start out that way. In 1936, the first science fiction "convention" was organized by SF fan and nuclear physicist, Dr. Milton A. Rothman. It took place at his house in Philadelphia. There were about fifteen attendees, including Frederik Pohl and David Kyle, another SF author. Only about half of the people there were from out of town. All from the Big Apple. In 1937, held at Bohemian Hall in Long Island City, the Second Eastern Science Fiction Convention saw about forty attendees. By the Fourth Eastern, in Newark, there were over 100. Finally, in 1939, the first World Science Fiction Convention took place in New York City, in conjunction with the World's Fair, welcoming attendees from around the globe. It's been going ever since, except during World War II. Now, whereas the con has mostly bounced around in the United States, it's also appeared in Australia, Canada, Germany, Great Britain, Japan, and the Netherlands. And the filkers have followed.

It didn't take much to set me and Jim off on a quest actually. Before the hunt for *Dark Star* began, and long before we ever heard of Ozoner, we went in search of a Cajun restaurant. Not a specific Cajun restaurant, mind you, just, *ya know?*, Cajun. Being in Columbus, Ohio, that probably sounds foolish, the Acadians not exactly known for their Midwestern residences. But since Jim wasn't a drinker, instead of engaging in the proud undergrad tradition of getting obliterated at bars and parties, we orbited Columbus on I-270 talking about the next restaurant we'd go to (when we weren't watching movies from North Campus Video, of course). Don't get me wrong, we weren't foodies. We preferred scarfing establishments, joints that served a preposterous amount of food where we could taunt each other into eating more, I mean after that *light snack* you just had, I'm sure you're up for dessert, what? no? how the mighty have fallen. So when Jim said he wanted Cajun, and seeing as how Columbus was expanding and expanding into the flatness of Central Ohio back in those days, having no natural borders, I-270 not exactly being a part of nature, we were positive we'd find one sooner or later.

We never did.

We were luckier with *Dark Star*, but that didn't mean it was easy. Thankfully, it wasn't. And much as we never found the Cajun restaurant we wanted, there were plenty of times we thought we'd never find the movie. But we kept looking, and that meant going to video rental joints...

There were, of course, the polished, mainstream shops (Blockbuster, Hollywood Video, Movie Gallery), where everything, somehow, felt like it was made of plastic. There were the local chains that did all they could to seem like the national chains. There were the one-offs that did the same thing. There were fortresses that had an insane amount of security, sensors at the doors, sensors on the tapes, high tech cameras and TV screens, a suspicious number of employees "restocking" shelves, the business ready at any time to turn your late fee into a misdemeanor petty larceny charge, though they definitely felt the justice system had let them down there, should be grand larceny, lock that son of a bitch up with the rest of the hardened criminals, just look at him, yeah, you can tell; and places that had a more laid back approach, fines being more in the vein of "this will hurt us more than it'll hurt you," if they bothered to collect the money at all. There were stores with a special room in the back where they kept the dirty movies, teenagers standing awkwardly just outside, *so close*, looking at SPECIAL INTEREST flicks, which were mostly exercise or how-to videos, as they tried to build up the courage to make it seem like they were old enough to go into that special room, just around the corner, hormones ablaze, why does this have to be so damned difficult, I mean *come on already* . . . There were mom and pop stores that definitely didn't have the dirty movie room. There were joints that either let you know a particular movie was available by having the VHS box on the shelf, or by having hard plastic boxes containing the tape behind the cardboard VHS container, or by the presence or absence of steel and paper tokens that hung beneath the cardboard VHS box. There were joints that didn't have the movies or the VHS boxes displayed, but instead had tiny posters with a description of the flick underneath and then slips of paper where you wrote your film down and took it up to the counter, and shops that had a bunch of binders with smashed VHS movie boxes in them, and you flipped through the binders to see if your movie was available. There were stores that were obviously intended to make money, had as many movies as possible, sparklingly clean, specials galore to keep people coming in, and joints that seemed to miss the boat on the whole capitalism thing, covered in dust, not sure if this is a business or someone's poorly curated collection, the one dude working there confused when you came in, not sure why you were asking him if they have whatever you were asking for, even more confused why you might be handing him a movie and some money, not sure when you were supposed to return the flick, less sure when they'd be open again, the Fifth of Never being maybe overly optimistic, seeing as how it at least sounds specific. There were joints that, like delivery restaurants, had menus of their movies, and you could call up and they'd bring the tape to you, though it was never entirely clear how you'd get it back to them, unless you physically showed up at the business, which begged the question why, if you have to get yourself there eventually, you didn't just do that in the first place? There were stores that specialized in foreign films, horror flicks, cult movies, video games (with the small, sad VHS collection off by itself), new releases (guarantees made that they'd always have a copy), and yes, dirty movies—though you didn't always know until you arrived, since they tended to have pretty innocuous names. There were even video stores combined with tanning salons, beauty salons, drugstores, head shops, pizza parlors, record stores, bookstores, and just about any other kind of business you can think of. And, in search of *Dark Star*, we went to all of them . . .

"No matter where you go, there you are," is what I learned from the first movie that was rented for me: *The Adventures of Buckaroo Bonzai Across the 8th Dimension*. It was in theatres in 1984, but I didn't get to see it then, for reasons long forgotten, so I had to wait until I was seven years old, the following year, when it was released on video. Now up to that point, I'd only seen movies in mall theatres, drive-ins, and on TV. I didn't know there was such a thing as video until my dad came home with a silver, front loading Sharp VC-581U VHS VCR. The buttons were colorful (green for PLAY, blue for STOP, red for RECORD). The remote had a cord, which might sound odd now, but it was the only remote we owned. My dad hooked up the VCR and told me about Video Channel, where he'd rented *Buckaroo Bonzai*. He told me they had all kinds of movies there, that I should make a list of the movies I wanted to see. When I asked if I could rent a movie, he said you had to pay for a club membership (something replaced later on by a credit card number they could charge if you decided a particular tape didn't need to be returned), that you had to pay for the rental itself, and you had to have a picture ID . . .

I zoned out once I started thinking about Video Channel. To my young mind, it wasn't just a repository of the movies that had been made, but all possible movies—everything you wanted to see could be found there. Much later, the standup comedian Steven Wright would tell a joke about trying to rent one of his dreams at a video store, and when the employees tell him that's not a movie, it's one of your dreams, he says, okay, let me know when you have it in. As I got older, I strangely continued to believe something like this every time I went into a new video rental store. This place, yes, this one, it will be the shop I've always imagined, the one that appears for me in my mind when . . . Of course, I was frequently disappointed. Consequently, wherever I lived, I cobbled together the best possible video rental store: in Munroe Falls, at different times, it was Ticket Stub, Network Video, Roadrunner Video, Blockbuster, and Hollywood Video; in Kent it was an amalgam of Video 101 (the closest thing to North Campus Video in my part of Ohio, though it was nowhere near as good as Magneto's joint), Movie Gallery, and Blockbuster. In Knoxville, it was Movie Gallery and, strangely enough, the public library (which had a phenomenal selection of art house and foreign films). But unlike what Buckaroo

Bonzai taught me, when it came to video rental stores, I was never in the place I was in. I was always somewhere else ...

... and if you don't mind, I'll join my younger self too, it being at least a decade since that impromptu performance on the porch in Tuscaloosa, me having lived in Chicago, Billings, and even Munroe Falls, where there's no longer a falls, just a Munroe, whatever that is, from then to now, though I can't promise you I'll remember every single last syllable, might have to hum along at certain points, chances of that happening: zero, like Cicero admitting he probably just invented Cato the Elder's oft-quoted refrain as a rhetorical flourish, unwilling to admit as much, like me unwilling to admit I, you know, maybe forgot, maybe invented some lines, nah, that right bastard Jameses II, he'd do something like that, but me? hell no, I know this song, you wait and see, and so I'm much more likely to sing what I think the words are, combobulated, discombobulated, recombobulated lyrics shouted with gusto, as if my version is the real version, what? those jerks up on the stage know better? ha! accuracy be damned ...

Karen Anderson is the first person to deliberately use the word "filk" in print; it appeared in *The Journal for Utter Nonsense* #774 (issue one having been arbitrarily numbered 771). Her article claims that "Barbarous Allen," a tune Poul Anderson, her husband, wrote, is "the first known song published as a filk song." Does that mean Karen Anderson invented the word? No. Instead, the term itself was accidentally invented when Lee Jacobs, an SF fan and zine publisher, wrote a piece in the 1950s titled, "The Influence of Science Fiction on Modern American *Filk* Music" (italics mine). The word Jacobs intended to use was, of course, *folk*. Wrai Ballard, editor of the Spectator Amateur Press Society's newsletter at the time, could have caught this mistake, but that was unnecessary, seeing as how he refused to publish the article, thinking the lewd lyrics contained therein would violate the Comstock Laws. Even though he didn't run the piece, the *filk* typo, that happy accident, was impossible for him to resist. Ballard and others, therefore, began to use it regularly. After a long, unintentional word-of-mouth campaign, Karen Anderson became the first to use what she thought was a generally accepted term in print, claiming her husband's song as "the first known song published as a filk song." The first filk song period? No. But with the qualification, I suppose she's right.

Me and Jim made a mistake too. After we finally saw *Dark Star*, we found we especially liked the song from the opening credits, so we'd sing it over and over again. For some reason, though, we thought the chorus was: "Benson, Arizona, it's where I want to be." Years later, when Jim road-tripped to Vegas with some Texan friends of his, he demanded that they stop in Benson. Since no one else had seen the John Carpenter movie, nor did they know the song, they weren't exactly sympathetic to or interested in this side-trek. Jim told them it wouldn't take long because he just wanted to get his picture taken next to a sign that bore the name of the town. Problem was, the signs for Benson weren't exactly situated so you could easily go and stand next to them, probably because Benson isn't exactly a tourist attraction. Undaunted, Jim began looking for postcards, souvenirs, really anything that had *Benson, Arizona* printed on it. No luck. With his friends getting annoyed, figuring every minute spent in this stupid desert town was a minute not spent in Vegas, Jim saw a Days Inn, ran inside, grabbed a business card and an envelope, wrote out our accidental addition to the Taylor/Carpenter song, and sent it to me, which prompted the time traveling, space bending sing-a-long.

Although I can't speak for Jim, that erroneous line has described my feelings rather frequently, especially when I moved to Billings, especially when I went to the only physical video rental joint in town and found desolation, and found the apocalypse had come, and found the ruin of my fantasies. Unlike with earlier movie stores, I didn't expect my dreams to be there. I expected nothing. And that's exactly what I got.

To protect the innocent, I'll call this place Post-Apocalypse Video.

There, the movies were organized alphabetically . . . sort of. There, the selection was broad . . . sort of. There, the categories on the shelves were helpful . . . sort of. There, the posters, the stand-ups, the atmosphere-creating film ephemera . . . there was none. There, the staff was . . . no one. You took your DVD to the grocery store style cash register aisles at the front and they rang up your purchase like you were buying toilet paper or zit cream or deodorant. Definitely no reason to start a conversation about *this* product. Just ferry these jerks on to the rest of their pathetic lives. The store was rather like a Best Buy that'd accepted the castoff merchandise of other now defunct Best Buys and had subsequently packed everything in, shoving the video rental section off into a back corner (why we do we even have this here?). An afterthought. I wandered through that wasteland on too many occasions, never once reviving the excitement I used to feel, always wondering why I'd bothered.

I'm told before it became Post-Apocalypse Video, that sad reminder of a glorious past was not only the best video rental joint in Billings, but maybe in all of Montana. Specializing in foreign films, it had over a thousand titles. But by the time I arrived, Post-Apocalypse Video made me wish I was somewhere else, anywhere else, even a place I'd never actually been before, even a place that likely doesn't exist at all as it does in my mind . . .

. . . *what we're doing now is we're waiting for the chorus to come back around, one more verse standing in the way before we join our champion, the self-styled Andysseus of the past there in Tuscaloosa, and our heel, the equally self-styled Jameses II (curse his name and his evil forces) of the further past there in Benson, though the threat imposed by either on the other is just as imaginary as the threat of Carthage on Rome, seeing as how Rome won the first two Punic Wars and then the third, giving the Italians a clean sweep, making Cato the Elder's fear that led to his constant refrain seem ludicrous, and a misworded and frequently used line referencing that fear more ludicrous still, but being fans of the obviously fictional and absurd, seeing as how we're set to sing a country-and-western song about space travel from a low budget movie, we'll celebrate that fandom right after this . . .*

From the 1950s to the early '70s, filking was an auxiliary activity at science fiction conventions. Normally meeting late at night in unused ballrooms, service passages, kitchens, hallways, stairwells, or really anywhere they could find space, the filkers were never the prime attraction. In fact, the whole enterprise was built on amateurism, since everyone who showed up and joined in the filking circle was encouraged to either perform (no matter their skill level) or sing along. Although the DIY vibe remains, in 1974, Bob Aspirin announced at the World Science Fiction Convention in Washington, D.C., the formation of the Dorsai Irregulars, an organized, though volunteer, filk band. More professional artists followed, such as Leslie Fish, who recorded the first commercial filk album: *Folk Songs for Folk Who Ain't Even Been Yet* (1976). Then, in the late '70s, periodicals dedicated to filk came about: *Kantele* and *Philk Fee-Nom-Ee-Non*. By the '80s, filk became an established activity at SF cons. Now, this musical style even has its own festivals, the most important being the Ohio Valley Filk Fest where the Pegasus Awards (like the Grammys for filkers) are given out. Although the OVFF began in Cincinnati in 1984, it moved to Columbus in 1986. Been held there every year since.

It wouldn't surprise me to learn that some filkers long for the day when their shows were purely amateur, long for how things used to be, much as a reader of this essay might assume I want the video rental joints to come back.

Each and every one of them. Including the boring ones. Including the lousy ones. But especially including the bizarre ones. Sure, why not? Makes sense. I mean, after all, me and Jim had to go on a quest to find *Dark Star*, to find Ozoner. These days, if we'd embarked on that same hunt, it would've required a few minutes, it would've taken us no farther than our own computers . . .

As filking goes, I can't tell you how anyone involved feels. Me and Jim never even attended the OVFF, though being held in Columbus every October, if we'd heard of it, a convention dedicated to folk music inspired by science fiction, fantasy, and horror, *are you kidding me?* and us always on the lookout for strange things to do, *hell yeah!*, we certainly would've gone.

But we never heard of it.

So we never went.

As for the video rental joints, well, me and Jim remember the end of our quest differently.

Jim's Version: "I don't know how we found Ozoner. I must have seen an ad for it somewhere because I otherwise had no business in that part of town and never went over there. I do remember the joy in finding the movie, but now I don't remember if I had seen it [on the shelf] first without you or if we found [the place and the movie] on a joint visit."

On the other hand, my version of the story is that our quest finally became desperate, that we wanted to see *Dark Star* so badly, a yearning created by its scarcity, that we began calling every video rental joint in the phonebook, every video rental joint in Central Ohio, to see if they had a copy. Only Ozoner did.

But revealing me and Jim have less than perfect memories, that's not the important part. The important part comes now. Because now is when I should tell you about Ozoner. I should describe this video rental Utopia. I should describe the folks who worked there. I should describe those who frequented this joint. I should, absolutely, describe the feeling the place instilled in me. Being a child of the '80s, I've seen so many of the movies and TV shows and *stuff* of my younger days return. Why not video rental? And to help resurrect my fantasies, here I should make you want Ozoner, I should make you yearn for it.

Only I'm not going to.

Instead, I'll say this: at one point in *Dark Star*, Lt. Doolittle, the acting captain of this beat-to-hell interstellar tin can, becomes nostalgic for surfing in California. The lieutenant even wishes he would've brought his board on the ship so he could just wax it occasionally. Throughout the movie we learn, though, that much of the earth is uninhabitable now (the disbanding of the Los Angeles Dodgers, the fact that a large colony of humans lives on Antarctica, the continued lack of any help from the home planet). Meaning? Meaning Doolittle couldn't surf even if he went back home.

And there's no returning to Ozoner either. From Jim: "The extra weird deal about it—I don't remember exactly where Ozoner was, and when I've gone back to Columbus and looked for it, the candidate building at that intersection looks different enough that I'm uncomfortable claiming it as the place."

Since Ozoner itself is gone, and since the Ozoner I remember has been manipulated by my memory, changed by my mind, I don't want anyone trying to recreate that place for me or anyone else, I refuse to aid in its reanimation, for then it'd only be the decaying, undead version of itself like so many other things I grew up with that shuffle, oozing and groaning, across the land now . . .

But even so, there are times when I like to think that Ozoner didn't go out of business, that it didn't fall into disrepair, that it didn't finally get knocked down and replaced by some other building. No, nothing so prosaic . . .

That's probably what happened, though.

And so, thanks to this conflict, of wanting this video rental store alive while willing to leave it behind, if I imagine Ozoner Video serving its purpose here on earth and then launching itself into space where it will continue to travel until another planet comes up on the radar that needs rare cult movies in the VHS and DVD formats, well then you will perhaps understand how someone could write nostalgic folk music influenced by science fiction.

Now everybody—

Hail Jameses II, Emperor of the Columns of Buseis, Slayer of the Dirty Rodents in That Land Up North, Son of Jameses I, King of the Lake in the West, Protector of the Mystical Trees of Day'vee.

In hilariously overwrought writing like this, we, through the electronic mail, lambasted each other with outrageous insults, made threats as grave as they were ambiguous, augured doom for the nonexistent forces commanded by the recipient, heaped great praise on ourselves for prowess in (fictional) warfare, in (actual) scholarship, in (strangely) peacekeeping. But then, just as it appeared we were the bitterest of foes, you and I would join forces, would battle (via Internet communiqués) against enemies real and fanciful, would celebrate yet another victory . . . until the hue of triumph and then peace began to fade—Treachery! Perfidy! Duplicity!—and thus the cycle would repeat. Amongst all of this, however, was another strain, one where we made great plans, plans for conquests of other universities, plans for grand journeys across this country, plans for epic expeditions abroad, plans to down as much as we could at legendary scarfing establishments, plans to raid the oddest video rental joints for the strangest movies imaginable that we would watch at times so late clocks wither envisioning them . . . yes, being so young, we looked to the future . . .

None of those emails survive. Neither do any of those video rental joints. And, really, all I want to say here is: sometimes, I miss them.

Well that . . . and I believe Carthage must be destroyed.

I remain,
Andysseus the Lost

Pool Hall Legend

See the pool hall.

Now, I'm not good at any billiards game, but I've spent enough time playing that I have my own image of the place. It's skeezy, with filthy, rutted wooden floors; row upon row of tables covered in beat-to-shit green baize, fragments of blue chalk cubes, shards of talcum powder towers; hooded lamps hanging low over the tables that create deep shadows, rather than help you see; racks of sticks that've almost become scythes; so much smoke you think the walls might ask you to run and grab them a carton of Lucky Strikes; ceiling fans that stir the atmosphere, instead of cooling it; a bar that serves whiskey, beer, and Boilermakers (a combination of whiskey and beer); a blackened, tin ceiling; and a clientele made up of bad dudes with scraggly beards wearing boots, blue jeans, flannel shirts or T-shirts, holding their own cues, sucking on cigarettes, eyeing any newcomer suspiciously.

But honestly, and you might be thinking this already, my image doesn't hold up. I mean, I've scratched on the eight ball in university halls, fluorescent lights buzzing from drop-ceilings overhead, surrounded by students who mostly don't know how to play (having grown up with video games); I've missed simple shots in yuppie hangouts, everything made to look plush and expensive: red felt, polished wood, faux-Tiffany lamps, pristine billiards bridges, framed pictures of gentlemen at snooker on the walls; I've miscued in entertainment complex rooms overrun by children rambunctiously cavorting between the lunar bowling alley, arcade, ping pong, Skee-Ball, and animatronic animal sectors; I've been six-packed (though no six-pack changed hands) in the 1990s update of the poolroom where there's no alcohol, no smoking, no gambling, no nothing but straight pool (they were trying to make Vegas family-friendly back then too); and I've sent balls over the rails and onto the floor in dive bars where the tables are shoved so far off in the corner you need a special tiny stick to shoot most of the shots.

And yet, if someone says "pool hall," even after taking a billiards course at Kent State (it fulfilled the phys ed requirement), where I learned the rules to an impressive number of cue sports I never played, where I was taught terminology I had no plans of remembering (especially after the instructor told us part of the table was called the Kitchen, which sounded like bullshit), where I otherwise played countless games of Cutthroat to pass the time, yes, even after all of this, if someone says "pool hall," still only one image enters my mind and only one story.

The image, you already have.

Here's the story (with some of the minor variants and guidelines on how to tell it):

You should be in the general vicinity of a billiard hall when you begin, so you can point to it as the impetus for the telling. You should say that a buddy of yours used to be a really good pool player, that he grew up with a table in the [basement or rec room], that you lost to him every single time the two of you played [maybe you beat him once, such a momentous occasion you can recall everything about that day even now]. You absolutely need to make clear that your buddy is a fine, upstanding member of the community [married, has kids, volunteers, goes to PTA meetings, a suburban saint] to set him off from the coming antagonist. "But one day" (it's very important to say it just like this, so we know the turn is here), your buddy decided he didn't want to play at home, so he went to a pool hall. Under no circumstances should you describe the pool hall. Let the listener fill in the details. With that "But one day" your auditor has already given the story such a terrifying setting, you could never top it anyway. Then pull a feint, "At first, everything was fine." Having found a good group, your buddy was shooting stick, he was having fun, he was winning (of course). Accentuate the fact that he was not winning *money*, however. The game has always been more than enough for him. Gambling actually ruins it. At some point, though, the romp had to end, so the group left, meaning your buddy was now by himself. And that's when he was approached by the stranger. You should not describe the stranger. The stranger is a shape-shifter, so no description would do him [it] justice. Do not tell your listener the stranger is a shape-shifter, though. Your listener will naturally make him a shape-shifter. Starting out, then, the stranger should seem pathetic. He's got no one to hang out with, asks your buddy if he would stay for just one more, and although it really was time to go, your buddy decided to play. Depending on how you want to tell this tale, when they start the game, it should be immediately apparent that the stranger is bad, though how bad is up to you. Maybe he misses the rack three consecutive times on the break, maybe he shoots at any old ball after the sides have already been determined, maybe he thinks the 8 is a solid like the 1–7. On the other hand, it could be that he's just unskilled. Whatever you decide, the fact of the matter is your buddy stomped him, plain and simple. Afterwards, the stranger may say any number of things: "I'm not usually this awful," or, "Wow! You're so good! Are you a professional?" or, "Did I win or did you win? I really don't know." But then comes the kicker, the line repeated, either verbally or mentally when, I'll bet, anyone at all thinks of pool halls:

"Do you want to play for money?"

Right here is the most important part in the story: a cut. You don't talk about your buddy wrestling with the ethical, or even moral dilemma of potentially taking a sucker's cash. You don't talk about your buddy accepting with a wolfish grin, or even with a resigned shrug, while mumbling the cliché about a fool and his money. You absolutely leave out any in-game details. Instead, you jump right to the ruinous end where your buddy dropped [insert outrageous amount here]; or he was cleaned out; or he not only lost what he had on him, he forked over the car, house, wife, maybe even the children, but after all that he's still in debt to the hustler, doubtful it'll ever be paid off, forced to run jobs for him the like of which you don't want to hear about, and if I haven't told you my buddy's name thus far, it's because, between you and me, I don't want to be associated with the bastard anymore.

I argue, some version of this urban legend has been passed around since the first pool hall opened.

But there are problems with it. First, sure, it seems likely, back before kids grew up playing video games in the basement instead of pool, that there *were* hustlers. How did they operate? These con men played on hubris. They knew you already thought you were good, figured you had an overinflated sense of *how* good because of all that time spent practicing in your basement or in your friend's rec room. After watching your opponent shoot poorly, then, you were absolutely ready to plunk your money down, or so the hustler hoped. But those days are long over. Meaning the marks don't exist anymore. As for the hustlers, again, I've shot in lots of different places over the course of twenty-five years, and yet there was only one time I ever thought someone was trying to bilk me. Honestly, even on that occasion I wasn't sure. In the end, I told the would-be swindler I don't play for money. And that was that. Consequently it seems we can say, by all evidence, that the marks are all gone and the hustlers have died out, so this cautionary tale continues on even after its usefulness is long over, a cultural-bound syndrome that refuses to vanish.

Another problem with the urban legend—it really seems to have a simple solution, one I've already explained (just don't play for money). But this is why the cut is so important to the story. Surprisingly, it doesn't seem to be a cautionary tale about avoiding hustlers. Instead, it seems to be a cautionary tale about *going into pool halls in the first place*. Inside the pool hall, *any* pool hall, according to this parable, the very nature of reality changes. It's bent, contorted, twisted beyond belief. And if you make the grave error of going inside one, you only have yourself to blame. And your punishment: you might lose some money, you might lose everything, you might even be damned. But nobody cares. Since it's all your fault.

Thanks to this story, I argue, we can't see pool halls. That's why the image that always comes to mind for me (and likely for you too) is one I've never actually witnessed. Because whatever we see on the inside couldn't possibly be real. Whatever our eyes take in, we know, is the purest form of mendacity. The truth of the place is buried under some kind of insidious witchcraft, obfuscated by a virtual simulation only a mad scientist could've invented. Without the use of our senses, we must intuit the interior of any pool hall. And that intuition, if working correctly, always lets us know to be on guard, no matter what the place happens to look like.

Though perhaps you disagree. Sure, you know the hustler story, but all that's over. Pool halls these days aren't anything special. They're just places where people play cue sports. Only, I'm now reminded of the Clive Barker-inspired film *Candyman* (1992). Helen, the protagonist, is studying graffiti, when she stumbles on a piece that references an urban legend which is dying out. Candyman, the spirit of the legend, near the end, contacts Helen and gives her an option. She can go about her life as per normal, or she can join Candyman in immortality by letting him kill her physical being. How would succumbing to this ghost allow her to live forever? Because her death would rejuvenate the legend of Candyman, and the two would continue on and on as more people believed in the story.

Now, you are faced with a similar situation. You can let things go the way they're going, you can let the mystique of pool halls die and be replaced by banality, or . . . you could play me. You know I'm oh so very bad. I'll even show you when you get here. All you have to do is come inside. That will be the moment of truth. Standing at the door. Deciding whether or not you'll go in. And if you do come inside, when the stakes are raised, after I ask, "Do you want to play for money?" you will find, having passed through the cut, that you must've said yes, because pool halls will have regained their haunting allure, and the characters in the cautionary tale will now have names, our names, and whereas the end of the story will show you ruined, you will not be ruined, because, thanks to this legend, you will join me in immortality in the pool hall.

I'll break.

Somewhere Better Than This Place

Gnostaloosa

They were tearing Tuscaloosa down. I never saw a single building demolished, never witnessed a wrecking ball, never observed a truck full of debris, never glimpsed a spud bar cracking away a doorframe, nor spied a jack or sledgehammer beat holes into the ground or into walls. But the city was coming down. That was certain. Everywhere were yellow vehicles parked next to rubble, next to great heaps of red dirt growing ever upwards into carmine dunes, and then parked on carmine flats, all of it progressing like a flipbook minus more than half the pages. An old movie that jumps too much, and that's missing an entire reel anyway. And I walked around and around the town, on an orbit trying to reach escape velocity, as this skipping, popping, jumping nickelodeon ran out. None of these buildings meant anything to me. And with each structure that disappeared, I hoped the real Tuscaloosa would emerge, the Tuscaloosa the Demiurge had obfuscated with strips of strip malls stripped of color, charisma, character.

I hoped a town would coalesce, I hoped a *city* would appear that I enjoyed, that I didn't want to flee. And there was reason to believe. Since I'd moved to Tuscaloosa people had been saying, "It might not seem like much now, but in the future . . ." [Insert a grand future here.] And that's what kept me holding on. That finally, this would be the place. . .

Outside of a high school that was being torn down, a very thin man approached me. The façade of the high school was still standing, but nothing else was.

"Big man! I don't believe we've ever met," he said.

His walk, as he approached, was springy, the walk of a cartoon cat. I agreed that I'd never met this man before, and when he asked my name, I gave the real one, though prone to giving fakes like Zane or Pablo when people I didn't quite trust inquired. And since he, the cartoon cat, didn't give a name, I thought of him as "Slick."

"Well, Andy, I'm here to tell you that I'm a native of Tuscaloosa, yes, I even attended that high school right there . . ."

He pointed to the façade of a school, or the school's façade, or both. It didn't seem to bother him that his alma mater was coming down.

"You mean . . . Central?" I said.

"Uh. . . Yeah!"

I thought about saying, "Go Wildcats!" or "Go Tigers!" and when he seconded, I'd point out that they were the Rebels and then be done with him, but I wanted to hear his story. I wanted it to be good. I imagined a character just in from a David Mamet play trying to con me as I walked down the street, and thought this could only be an improvement, this could only be an avatar from the real Tuscaloosa.

"What do you do?" said Slick.

"I'm a fiction writer." This isn't the kind of answer I normally give, but on this occasion, where it was so obvious we were working with whole cloth, I decided to admit that I was a bullshitter, too, accentuating the bullshitting nature of my own profession, hoping this would encourage Slick, nay, would inspire Slick on to greatness.

Then Slick went on to say that he worked for an independent television or film company, I was never quite sure which, and that he wanted to give me a job (a surprise I hadn't expected, optimism for Slick and his cockamamie scheme building), that the job would pay about $500, and all I would have to do is show up to the set on Saturday, that really the job was just standing since I was to be an extra in the piece being filmed, and that perhaps a guy like me could use $400 or $500, especially for, like, just an afternoon of, *you know?*, standing.

"Are you interested? Are you intrigued?" Slick said.

I admitted I was (although after the mistake with the $400 I was getting nervous).

And then Slick shifted gears. He came to the turn of the story, where after laying the ground situation (works for a video company, wants to give me a job), he had to admit that if a problem was not taken care of, our tale may become a tragedy. He said he'd locked his keys in his van. That all of his equipment was in the van. And that if he couldn't open the van and get to the equipment, then he couldn't film the whatever it was he wanted to film on Saturday.

And if he couldn't film, I (and this would be sad, no, it would be wrong) I couldn't make my, like, $300 or $400. And a man like me . . . Not to mention, continued Slick (piling another problem on top of the previous that could also lead to tragedy), that his brother had run into trouble with the law. That his brother was the producer. And if Slick couldn't get his brother out, then . . .

So what Slick was trying to say was, in order for this story to have a happy ending, where he (Slick) in concert with his brother (the Producer) filmed the who-knows-what wherein I appeared as an extra who would totally be making at least $200 if not more, for this to happen, Slick needed an advance of $50, which I would be making back on, *you know*? Saturday, along with the afore-mentioned . . . And if I don't have fifty, any amount would be fine.

I stopped walking.

I looked away.

My faith in Slick was pretty much gone. He'd really have to pull off a mira-cle to get me back.

And Slick slowed his cartoon cat strut. And he turned around.

He seemed grave.

And then, minus the pizzazz he'd displayed earlier, maybe understanding he needed to hit this one out of the park, he spoke.

Slick said:

"Come on, *big* man. Could you *make up* a story like this?"

Slick wasn't so slick anymore.

I said:

"Remember when I told you I'm a *fiction* writer?"

Slick began hemming and hawing, mumbling, clearing his throat, said all he wanted to do was help a guy like me make $100 or so, and then he fell on that old saw: "My car broke down in another part of town, and I need $30 for gas money, could you help me out?" as if I hadn't been along with him the en-tire way, listening, listening to him construct a world that'd never come to be.

I shook my head.

And Slick briskly walked off, no longer a cartoon cat, saying over his shoul-der: "Pray for me, big man, cuz I need help."

Behind me now, I thought of the school that was being torn down, hopefully soon the true source of knowledge would be revealed, an academy filled with wisdom, where intelligence flowed broader and faster than the Black Warrior

River, and I could see this very academy in the Tuscaloosa of the future, the student body standing on a manicured lawn, the teachers for some reason in those old-fashioned (probably never *in* fashion) caps and gowns, everyone smiling and waving, waving, and then there's a camera, it's a commercial for the academy, it's the filming of the commercial, and I'm standing in the back, an extra, but unlike the rest I'm unsmiling, unwaving because I can see who's directing the TV spot, and I know there's not going to be any $500 or $300 or any hundred dollars for my appearance.

Breaking the reverie someone offered to give me a ride. Because no one walks in Tuscaloosa. In this heat. They (the motorists) couldn't believe their eyes. *Someone walking. In this heat. In Tuscaloosa.* Whoever heard of such a thing! But I forged on. On my own. Blazing through this poorly constructed falsity toward something better.

Crimson Transmission

I used to say:

It is true, this place, this Tuscaloosa is blocking me from the existence I crave. But up the street, yes right up Hackberry Lane, there is proof that something better is out there. Here a group of Aeons labor toward the good.

Perhaps I didn't use those exact words . . .

But up the street from me was a decrepit mechanic's shop. And I wondered how it could still be open. I thought maybe it was a scam, that most auto repair joints were scams, that most mechanics were Archons, were con artists to some extent.

The shop was called Crimson Transmission, and the sign had a picture, so inexplicable, of a bear that resembled the bears on Grateful Dead bumper stickers. The man behind the counter, covered in grease, all grime, every crevice, every pore, smoked cigar stubs that were never full cigars; he made me think that him and the boys appeared one day, materialized from the red dirt, sauntered out of heat waves shimmering up from the asphalt road, figured this building would be a good front, a good way to collect cars from the unwitting yokels and the fatuous undergrads, cars that'd later be fixed up somewhere, somewhere else, anywhere else, and then they'd sell 'em. Make a mint. The lobby where I met the grease golem was full of rundown furniture even my old fraternity house would've junked after using it for a front lawn party set, it was full of vending machines that hadn't sold so much as a stale Clark bar to anyone within my personal lifetime, it was full of and everything was coated with black dust. It smelled like an electrical fire and gear oil.

When I dropped my car off there, the 1992 Mercury Cougar, I told the grease golem what was wrong, and in this age of computers he looked at me, skeptical, as if I might be speaking in a cipher intended to spell certain doom for him and his kind, as if I might be there to uncover his hoax, and then he took the cigar stub out of his mouth, out of his mouth when I'd gotten to thinking it was attached, and he said, "Shoot, I better write this down," and when he couldn't find a pen, he asked to borrow mine. Wrote down what I said, nodding sarcastically. Challenging me. Challenging me to call his bluff, to expose his racket. Challenging me because he didn't think for one goddamned second that a guy with clean, callous-free hands was going to bring down the curtain on his operation . . .

But they didn't steal my car. They fixed it. And cheap. And the place remained open. And instead of thinking that it might vanish overnight, the boys taking their ill-gotten gains with them, I began to see into the future, a future forever and always populated by citizens in silver jumpsuits driving hovermobiles, living in sleek, sword-like towers, a future lit by blue halogen lights and digital billboards, and there, in the background, with it all, would be that holdover from the 1950s, maybe the '30s, the filthy mechanic's shop, how could it still be here?

Then Crimson Transmission was gone. Evaporated into a smoothed lot of red dirt. I never saw a single semi or steamroller, not a back-hoe or a Bobcat, but it was gone. I tried to imagine it transcending this realm, becoming a crimson beam, a transmission sent to somewhere better than this place. But looking at the miniature field of red dirt surrounded by a fence, I really couldn't. And it was then that I began to think Tuscaloosa couldn't be transcended. It could only be endured. That each building that came down didn't reveal the Truth. It was only a void, a void where something used to be. And now there was nothing. And when people asked me to describe Tuscaloosa I said, "There's really nothing here." And, like strip malls and cul-de-sac neighborhoods elsewhere, the nothing was expanding.

Absurdaloosa

Outside my apartment an off-white Ford Ranger (maybe it was just white once) striped thick red and yellow between the wheels came to a squeal-grinding and hiccoughing stop. The two maintenance men, one the elder, paunchy, a bit stooped, with a gray mustache, the other taller, more muscular (although still fleshy), with random acts of curly beard and head hair, ambled into my driveway, stretched, spoke of something of little interest to each, their mouths barely moving, their heads nodding, performing a compulsory routine observed by hidden strangers only paranoiacs acknowledge. Then they, the maintenance men, moseyed to the door.

There was a long pause. Possibly a continuance of the coerced routine. Then a knock.

They'd been to my apartment before. When my sink was clogged, the maintenance men arrived, looked at the sink, looked at each other, looked at the sink again, said, "Clogged . . . Yep, clogged"; after a driving rainstorm when the floor in my office was soaked, they arrived, felt the floor, said, "Wet," looked at the back of the duplex, looked at each other, long pause, and then: "rotten boards"; and for the other miscellaneous troubles with the apartment, the maintenance men would arrive, look at the what-have-you, look at each other, back at the deal, back at each other, and declare that something was wrong, yep, something was wrong, and then they would meander away, as if this was their job, to witness the things that had gone wrong with the world and to acknowledge that, indeed, things do go wrong. Each time, then, after they left, I, assuming they were coming back to fix, to troubleshoot, to repair, or maybe even to jury-rig, would wait until it was obvious they weren't returning, so I'd call again, stating this time I wanted the problem, right? taken care of, not, you know, merely diagnosed.

But on this occasion the maintenance men had been summoned because I reminded my landlady that, unlike the other apartments, I didn't have a dishwasher. So the duo arrived. And they looked at the place where the dishwasher should be. They looked at the hookups where the dishwasher, if one were handy, would hook up. They seemed to confer through eye movements, gestures, nods, a recondite body language I would never decipher. Then the elder said, "No dishwasher." The other slowly shook his head in agreement.

They prepared to leave.

"But . . . But . . . Where are you going?"

"No dishwasher," the elder repeated.

"Will you . . . uh . . . be bringing one, you know? back . . . here?"

They said something I couldn't make out, shrugged, and left.

I stood, looking at the place where a dishwasher ought to be, but wasn't. And I decided to go for a walk. Down past the former site of a strip mall that contained a church and a florist, but which was now a square of red dirt surrounded by a fence, a car stopped next to me, and from inside: "You're walking." I paused, then agreed. "In this heat." I paused, then agreed. "In Tuscaloosa." Delayed agreement continuing. "In the Tuscaloosa heat, you're walking." I thought maybe it was the maintenance men in disguise, until the driver followed up with, "Wanna ride?" But I didn't.

Walking on, I imagined myself at the University of Alabama Arboretum, which I called Apocalypse Park because it had been a golf course and still resembled a golf course except that it was overgrown with weeds and thistles and crab grass and the greens and the fairways were the same as the rough, it was a golf course after the landscapers had died off, and now it was a park with a hiking trail which was the former cart track. I decided that the town wasn't being torn down, no, it was crumbling, and since the Mayor couldn't do anything about it, he'd decided to deploy yellow vehicles next to the ever growing piles of rubble and debris, next to the carmine dunes, each structure that came down making it tougher on the Mayor's story that a new Tuscaloosa was coming, that a brave new Tuscaloosa would arise in . . . the future, and as each building keeled over into its usual pile of detritus, as the last building in Tuscaloosa cascaded to the ground, I imagined an off-white Ford Ranger pulling up into Apocalypse Park, red and yellow stripes, unhealthy automobile sounds, a duo of men ambling, stretching, repeating a routine performed for those of the shadow world, mandated by those of the shadow world, the two maintenance men, not there to fix a damn thing, no, the two maintenance men had been called in to be witnesses to it all.

Samuel Beckett's Laundromat

I went into the Cleansing Tide Laundromat, everything in Tuscaloosa being named after the university's Crimson Tide in some way, wondering how it was that in a town where my friends had regularly been screamed at by passing motorists (cyclists often called faggots, gals got catcalls (some lewd, some just whistles), miscellaneous striders given the classic "fuck you" or "loser," the best instance being a friend who was looking at a book while shuffling down the sidewalk and someone from an SUV shouted, "Stop reading while you're walking, bitch!"), well how could it be that I kept getting offered rides by complete strangers?

I'm interrupted by a pained sigh. In stereo.

This wasn't new. Anytime a customer came in, especially the ones who used the drop-off service (as I did), the ladies at the counter gave a deep, deep sigh. On occasion they even said, "You, again?" no matter how long it'd been since my last visit.

On this occasion there were two women behind the counter. Both old. Giving the impression that they were ancient. That they'd been around since women beat laundry against rocks while men stabbed food with spears.

"How are you today?" I said.

"Can't complain."

"Can't complain."

"Could complain."

"Yep."

"But no one'd listen."

"Nope. No one."

"Even if they did, no one'd do anything."

"Just the way things are."

"Yep."

"Same thing every day."

"Doesn't change."

"More things change . . ."

"What changes?"

"More things stay the same, more things stay the same."

"Doesn't change. No changes."

Beat.

"Look."

"What?"

"A blue truck."

"A blue truck?"

"Another. Blue. Truck."

It was then that I knew what would be built in the lots of red dirt. It was then that I knew, if I walked up the road, someone would offer me a ride. Because it had happened before. So it would happen again.

Tuscaloosa 2: The Revenge

Earlier in the day I'd seen them rebuilding Central High School. And maybe it didn't look exactly like it did before. But for the most part, it was the same. There was nothing interesting about the new place. Anyone who saw it, even if the sign had been blown over by a gale-force wind, would say, "I bet that's a school." Yes, Tuscaloosa was repeating. Only I didn't want it to repeat. I wanted a city of the future. I would've taken a dystopian, postapocalyptic wasteland. I refused to believe that it was all just going to happen again.

Then I heard a voice.

It said:

"Big man! I don't believe we've ever met." I looked up. It's the very thin man walking like a cartoon cat.

Tired, there in the past, I say, actually, we have met. I say, you graduated from Central High School, a school that's been torn down and rebuilt, but you probably wouldn't notice because you couldn't remember what it was called the last time we talked, and because it looks pretty much the same. I say, you work for an independent film or television company, I'm not sure which because you kept that ambiguous, among other things. I say, probably you'll offer me a job, but all your equipment'll be locked in your van.

"Uh . . . oh."

"Then you're gonna ask me for money."

"Well, I wasn't going to ask you for money."

"You weren't?"

Beat.

"Uh . . . no."

"Then what can I do for you?"

"Uh . . . what time is it?"

"I dunno. Does it matter?"

"No. I guess not."

And he strode off, devoid of his cartoon cat walk again. And I looked around. At the buildings that surrounded me. At the vacant lots that surrounded me. Yesterday there were buildings in the lots and lots where there were now buildings. And tomorrow? I didn't need any imagination. I didn't need to be a prophet. I was one of the maintenance men; I'd never realized. But I wasn't there to witness destruction. I was there to witness this present: the future. And the experience was to be static. It would never change.

A Front or Affront

Sometimes I believe that this less material life is our truer life, and that our vain presence on the terraqueous globe is itself the secondary or merely virtual phenomenon.

—*H.P. Lovecraft*
"Beyond the Wall of Sleep"

I t is common in cosmic horror stories for characters to seek forbidden lore in aged, inhospitable places, to study the arcane wisdom found there, to see reality anew on account of this eldritch knowledge, and then to be driven mad. But I have gone, have studied, have seen (and still see) the world like few others ever have, and yet I am not mad. I, contrary to the beliefs of my detractors, am gloriously sane. What follows, then, is an account of my journey and a correlation of my mind's contents, one that has taken me many years to assemble. I must warn you, however, this essay, encroaching upon the boundaries of the macabre, contains no beauty; it *does* contain the sublime—two concepts which Immanuel Kant separates this way: the beautiful elicits "a pleasant sensation, but one that is joyous and smiling," while the sublime "arouse[s] enjoyment, but with horror." And there *will* be horror. So I understand if you leave now. Furthermore, as a doctor of knowledge, it is to be assumed that I am better prepared for assaults upon my mental faculties, am capable of holding diametrically opposed ideas in my mind without breaking, an ability that is essential since here I am working with the division between the real and the fantastic, a division hardly as stalwart as you might believe. For instance, the working title of this piece was "In Defense of Fronts," as in "front company," a defense I intend to lay before you, a defense I intend to make because I now believe the Front is the most honest form of business, though I know it to be dishonest to the core, making it sound to the unqualified like I am deranged, having accepted a completely fictional world as real, making it sound as if I belong in an institution for the criminally insane, though I am not insane. Append the fact that I will be using three Kent, Ohio, comic book stores (two dead, one alive if not exactly kicking) to make my point and the fact that I will be writing in a form (creative nonfiction) that is popular, if very fraught, and certainly it would be better if you did absolutely anything else with your time. After all, this piece is likely not for you. But for those who continue on, if reality should begin to warp and twist around you, if you should begin to doubt your senses, understand, *you have been warned.*

The Rodney Compleat Bookshoppe is precisely the kind of place that would appear in a cosmic horror story. Located on Water Street in Kent, it sounds as if it were situated in the Old World. Though downtown, I grew up during a time when downtown was not necessarily where you wanted to go, where you expected to find what you were looking for. Instead, this central portion of the city was a ramshackle collection of buildings, many of which served dubious or inexplicable purposes (except for the many taverns that served the usual obvious purpose). If you walked past the Compleat Bookshoppe without seeing it, that would be no surprise; if you stood at the door in the light of day and thought it was closed, though the posted hours said otherwise, that would be even less of a surprise. The very essence of the Compleat Bookshoppe is the copper's line: "There's nothing to see here."

Standing outside, however, I am reminded of Phillips Men's Store in Akron, Ohio, across the street from Chapel Hill Mall, for that was my introduction to the Front. My father initiated me into this knowledge, and he did so by describing the boutique semi-frequently, a description that would always include the following details: (1) all of the suits in the shop were covered in at least an inch and a half of dust, (2) it smelled strongly of mildew and rot, (3) at first glance, the establishment appeared to be abandoned, until (4) you ventured deep into the recesses of the building and found the eternal, illegal card game in the smoky backroom, (5) the players of cards were never happy to see you and made you fear for your life, (6) if you *did* convince someone to help you . . . but no, that was impossible, unthinkable. Finally, each time my father told this story, he would conclude with: "You know that place has just *gotta* be a front."

I admit, I always enjoyed hearing my father deliver this oration, though I merely thought it was humorous and nothing more. In fact, I fully intended to visit Phillips Men's Store when I was old enough to drive to see what it was actually like. I never did. Instead, I remembered what my father had said and, perhaps unconsciously, added my own elements to the sketch[1]; little did I realize that the Front, although maybe only in a minor way, had already begun manipulating my reality.

What surprised me as my father laughingly talked about this suspicious shop, however, was that his sarcasm seemed more bitter than jovial. And when he reached the final line, without fail, he appeared angry that such a place could exist and go on existing.

Confused at the time, it wouldn't be until I was forty years old and walking past the Rodney Compleat Bookshoppe that I briefly knew why my father was bitter, angry. Or, I should say, I thought I knew. Spellbinders, my favorite comic book store, was dead. Watch the Skies!, perhaps the best comic book store I'd ever been to, was long gone. But the Compleat Bookshoppe, with its broken racks in the window, with its browned and curling comics sitting on those racks (comics that weren't worth a red cent in the first place), with its idiotic name on that preposterous, old-timey sign (it's a comic book store, not a soda fountain), yes, the Compleat Bookshoppe, like some ancient, malevolent god sent to disseminate despair, disgustingly remained. Right then, I understood when my dad described Phillips, he was unable to keep himself from remembering all the places he'd ever loved and how they'd been devoured by time, while this hellhole somehow persisted, a blight on reality so hideous, even the visions and works of occultists from cosmic horror stories could never compare, in fact, only the machinations of a character from one of those tales in league with some unknowable evil entity could facilitate the persistence of Phillips or the Compleat Bookshoppe.

I was angry.

But I'm not angry anymore.

(The world looks so different to me now, as if I weren't just seeing with my eyes . . .)

For certainly the Compleat Bookshoppe did not send, say, Watch the Skies! into obscurity. Rodney's store, after all, is a version of The Front, while Watch the Skies! was an avatar of The Flare.

No matter where you happen to reside, you've likely had this experience: a new business opens in town, but instead of being yet another crass, commercial venture, it turns out to be, dare I say, *awe-inspiring*. Immediately, you wonder how, in a world of aggressive banality, where bathos is so powerful it might as well be an ethereal ectoplasmic leviathan that has engulfed the entire planet, raining a beige ooze upon the lot of us, a beige absorbed by our skin, seeping into our bloodstreams, slushing our organs, corrupting our bones, until it claims our very essences, an essence of beige transforming us into beige beings, *how*, in that world, populated by those galoots, could a place like The Flare exist? At the grand opening (the first time you actually agree with the use of "grand," instead of thinking it ironic, painfully, painfully ironic), when you finally walk through the doors, the sensation is so puissant, it makes you believe the world has finished sloughing off dull detritus on us, it makes you (gasp!) optimistic. Whatever The Flare might be for you, you stare, astonished, full of wonderment, upon its glory (another shockingly un-ironic usage!). From then on, you go as much as you can, you bask in the grandeur, you look at your friends, your family, and without using words you say, "Can you believe this? I mean, can you believe it?" and they can. Barely, but they can. For everyone loves The Flare.

This was Watch the Skies! (the exclamation point in the name did not seem merely necessary, but essential). A pristine comic book store, it carried everything you could imagine and more, was owned by a DC Comics artist who worked in an amazing studio on the second floor loft; there was even a giant, intricate sculpture of a UFO which had ostensibly slammed into one of the interior brick walls with a television jutting out from underneath that broadcast images perhaps to its home world. Standing in Watch the Skies!, I felt as if I had been abducted, taken away from Kent, from Ohio, and had been delivered to another dimension, a better dimension, a *superior* dimension.

For Immanuel Kant, this is the splendid sublime. Why sublime and not beautiful? Because, of course, following the venerated tradition of The Flare, in no time, the place closes down. No explanation. Not even any rumors. Just closed. Perhaps, as you uncomprehendingly try the door, you see a beige ooze stuck to your hands … before it vanishes. Maybe the building, with an impossible immediacy, appears decayed, weathered, dilapidated, as if it existed long ago, as if you'd dreamed the entire experience and that dream was over, as if perhaps it never really was at all. The tragic nature of The Flare's character is what makes it sublime. If Watch the Skies! were alive, or even if it'd had a long life, we might be able to call it beautiful. Instead, our memories are tinged by the horror of death, a death that came way too soon.

(But then, from in here, I can see Watch the Skies! as if it still were, I can see places that are better, and I can see places that are far worse than the Compleat Bookshoppe, and you can too if . . .)

To compare The Flare and The Front is unfair. With its scuffed tile, its clutter (but what *is* all this junk?), its dust, its racks that appear perpetually on the verge of keeling over, its boxes (have they just moved in? will they vanish into the night leaving only rumors in their wake?), the atmosphere is repellent[2], perhaps purposefully so. Back when The Flare was open, on the other hand, it was oh so inviting . . .

But the Compleat Bookshoppe isn't the next type either: The Dive. Whereas everything was perfect about The Flare (save for its untimely demise), nothing is perfect about The Dive, yet neither the employees, nor the patrons would have it any other way. Dark, disorganized, likely dirty, whereas avatars of The Flare are uncommon, The Dive exists in copious amounts. Entering one unconsciously is like stumbling upon a secret cultist shrine. Unlike world religions, here the adherents, who I love wholeheartedly, are unhappy to see you, evidenced by their heavy sighs (which I also love). When in service to their master, see them fly; when in service to you, everything requires so much effort, too much effort, Herculean effort even, evidenced by another round, even another chorus of the heaviest of sighs. It is truly remarkable that, as these acolytes talk amongst themselves, their intelligence is vast, but with you, they have no knowledge at all about the paltry offerings in the store, or they willfully withhold information about the overly vast stock. If nothing seems quite right about The Dive, that's because it's not supposed to . . . unless you become one of the cultists yourself. From the outside, one can only imagine that these poor souls want nothing more than to go out of business and be free of this place, but somehow, against their best efforts (or utter lack of effort), they continue on. I like to imagine, at the end of the year, whilst going over the books (which I see as actual, dust-covered books, not slim, futuristic computers or tablets), the employees learn that, yes, they somehow, someway made a profit. After this announcement there is a pause. A long, long pause . . . Followed by a collective sigh. The heaviest of sighs. Hercules himself would've been crushed by this sigh. And with finality, one person in the back, who likely collapses from the exertion, says, "Goddamnit." And business trudges forth. The shrine won't let them leave, ostensibly. From the inside, however, and I can tell you because I have seen the inner sanctum, from the inside: the cultists don't want to go under, they *want* to be there.

1990s Kent had a version of The Dive called Spellbinders. Although it was not in a basement, you entered from the parking lot by descending one outdoor staircase, then, inside, another, making you feel like you were far underground, making you wonder if the windows at the front of the store were actually looking out onto reality, or onto something else entirely. The general ambience, with its intermittent lighting, its deep shadows, its walls of terrifying costumes, its constantly-in-flux display cases featuring bizarre items intended for unknown (perhaps unknowable) uses, yes, the general ambience was that of an antiquities shop from a horror story, where one could purchase *anything* for the right price . . . and that price might not include any specie, if you get my meaning. And whereas the owner and the manager were standup individuals, the employees, the true disciples of this comic and game store, were more than happy to stare into the middle distance, to speak of the purposefully esoteric to exclude non-adepts, to hide from the customers in the hermetic sanctuary devoted to their alien deity.

This, I argue, is what Kant calls the noble sublime. Spellbinders was never beautiful, never tried to be beautiful, and thank goodness for that. And when we compare The Dive to the rest of the businesses in the world, with quiet wonder we admire how many iterations there are, even though the atmosphere is uninviting, even though the locations are relatively obscure, even though the workers are indifferent or even mildly annoyed at the concept of customers. It could be that each installation of The Dive is an extraterrestrial experiment, or maybe even a taunt: "You seem to believe that everyone and everything needs to be in constant competition. But here, the only competition is who can care less about your petty competitions." By the rules of capitalism, no avatar of The Dive should live on. But they do.

(Though it appears nothing is here, everything is here, you just need the right eyes to see with . . .)

At first blush, The Dive and The Front appear analogous, but they are not. The clutter and gloom, the relative indifference to customers at The Dive is there to drive dilettantes away, while welcoming in the neophytes. The Front, on the other hand, wants to admit no one, wants to keep no one. Should you ever get the chance, when you finally enter and meet Rodney (if that is even the name of the person "working" there, or perhaps "employed" there, or perhaps just *is* there, so, when you finally enter and meet *Pseudo*-Rodney)[3], and he persistently and skillfully, in league with the place itself, directs you elsewhere, convinces you that this is not the comic book store you were looking for, then you will understand The Front is nothing like The Dive.

Because The Front . . . The Front is different. With The Flare and The Dive, with really any business, what's important are the iterations themselves. That's not the case with The Front. So whereas we could say any number of things about where a particular avatar is located, what it's like inside and out, the most important aspect is the fact that it seems like it's never open, even when the sign on the door says it is. And the likelihood of you or anyone you know having entered is almost nil. But even if you had, if this is a true version of The Front, you wouldn't be able to see anything. Why? Beforehand, you would've heard the conjectures, the obviously told and retold tales, the urban legends, including details about how nobody's ever seen going in or out, about mysterious deals, about secret basements and sub-basements, about trucks delivering shipments in the dead of night, about the owner's missing spouse or even missing family, about how no one's laid eyes on the *actual* owner in years, or that maybe the owner's a phantom himself or herself, about how the place never seems to be open and yet it doesn't go out of business, about this strange smell that billows out from the cellar, about that light, oh that unnerving light, nothing natural makes a light like that, and the building's bathed in it throughout the eventide. The stories always end with, "You know that place has just *gotta* be a front," the implication being a front for the mob, no one saying which mob, or acknowledging the complete lack of a real mob presence in this town in the first place. But that is inconsequential because The Front cannot be The Front if it is proven to be a front, or if it is proven to be anything at all. Unproven, ill-defined, unknown, always extending beyond our capacity to fully imagine it, to fully understand it, growing mammoth, monstrous in our minds, while still unassuming in its physical form, intimidating not our persons, but our psyches with its ethereal rhizomatic expansion, this is why, even if you went inside, you still wouldn't see The Front, because much as Pseudo-Rodney tries to divert you elsewhere, each atom inside redirects your attention to an elementary explanation that annihilates the corporeal entity before you and replaces it with a host of comfortable fictions you pretend are the real reality.

But you can't lie to yourself any longer.

Before, about dying businesses, you could say, "This place's time has come and gone"; for The Front, you will say, pleadingly, "This place's time never was and will never come to be." Yet it's here before you.

And now, confronted with this grotesque, beset by this inextricable mixture of the fictional and nonfictional that has destroyed your vision of the universe, having finally (perhaps accidentally, perhaps inadvertently) found your way inside (you *were* warned), you might wonder why anyone would seek out Kant's terrifying sublime, imbued with dread and melancholy as it is. If these are your thoughts, Pseudo-Rodney will try to save you by strategically, ingeniously, even aggressively making it seem like nothing can be accomplished here, nothing can be found here, nothing can be done here, nothing can be learned here, nothing can be known here, because the Compleat Bookshoppe *is not for you.* After Pseudo-Rodney makes everything seem impossible, though, he will say (and, if you don't mind, I will say it for him) that everything is only impossible *here*. Away, away from this place there is an entire world of achievement, a *real* world, you need merely step over the threshold to be in it.

If you are like me, you will be suspicious of Pseudo-Rodney, suspicious that something simpler can be found outside, something real, for the simple real is a dream; actual reality is the terrifying sublime. And now you will seek it out by joining me in the Compleat Bookshoppe, where people stare in confusion when the door is locked during operating hours, where the world warps and twists for as long as it continues on.

If you aren't like me, though, when you enter (*how did you get in?*), I won't correct you when you call me Rodney. Instead, I will warn you about what might happen in here, I will initiate you into the forbidden lore of The Front, and then, to save you, to let you off the hook, I will say: you can trust me because, of everyone on earth, I alone am sane. Gloriously sane. I know, I know. In the past, you have only heard crazy people use that line. And in the past, you were right: they were crazy. But that's because none of them were me, the only sane person there is. Back outside, for a moment, your reality slightly warped, you might wonder if I am not actually deranged, if the things I said were true. A scary thought . . . Then everything will smooth, your simple explanations will return, "The only sane one! Right!" and you can move on through the beautiful new downtown of Kent, Ohio, the solid city, the straightforward city, the verifiable city, the (perhaps most importantly) comprehensible city that surrounds you, that streams by as you walk, that shares nothing in common with and therefore never calls to mind again the Compleat Bookshoppe.

Notes

1. Here, I feel it necessary to say this form I'm working in, creative nonfiction, although fraught, is the most popular genre in and outside of the academy. And the reason I believe creative nonfiction is so popular: because people in general have trouble with fiction, are leery of fiction, are even suspicious of fiction.

NB It's common for students to confuse authors and their narrators. When informed that these two entities are *not* the same, the students nod politely and studiously, though the barely withheld smirks tell the real story: "We'll pretend for you, teacher guy, but we know better. I write about myself, everyone in history has written about themselves, why don't you just admit it?"

NB₂ It's common for people who happen to read an *odd* or *weird* work to use either or both of these responses: "X must've done some really [good/bad] drugs" or "What drugs did X do?" The reason these responses are so popular: because they immediately throw us back into the comfortable realm of personal experience. I am consequently working on a class called "Authorship and Pharmacology," wherein we will read various works of *strange* fiction, we will study the effects of various drugs, we will determine which drugs or which combination of drugs our favorite authors took, and we will then ingest that drug/those drugs so we can write like our favorite *bizarre* authors.

NB₃ It's common for people to say that they care too much about reality to waste their time with fiction. Don Hertzfeldt, for instance, after presenting his animation at the Music Box Theatre in Chicago, when asked what fiction he read, said that he didn't read fiction because, at some point, he realized that none of what he was reading was real, it was just something someone made up. Granted, I stopped myself from responding with a pointed lie about how I didn't like animation for similar reasons.

Creative nonfiction, on the other hand, requires the writer to focus on reality, so none of the problems with fiction arise. Yes, the authors are frequently writing about themselves. Yes, if the authors have taken drugs, they'll likely tell you about it. And Don Hertzfeldt needn't worry: when you're reading creative nonfiction, it's not just something someone made up.

2. I have said two times that creative nonfiction is fraught, and so it is. Although popular, the name, a collision of words that appear to be antonyms, *creative* and *nonfiction*, puts most people off. Once, I had an editor accept my work by saying, "To be honest, when I see 'creative nonfiction' in an incoming message, it's generally not a good sign." The problem is that *creativity*, many believe, leads to invention, while *nonfiction* is reporting on or otherwise delineating the truth. The other names don't fare well either, though. *Memoir*, in the singular, is detested for sounding pretentious, while *memoirs* are only acceptable from historically significant persons (unless the

personage in question fails to pronounce the "r," in which case they are even more pretentious). *Essay* calls to mind what students have to write in high school and college, and who wants to read a collection of high school and college essays? Not even the instructors who assigned them. *Personal essay*, much like *creative nonfiction*, sounds like words are just being slapped together again pell-mell. *Journalism* might be acceptable, except that it's quite specific, and therefore not a big enough umbrella. The word *nonfiction*, on its own, is popular, but has the opposite problem of *journalism*—it's so big, saying you prefer to read nonfiction is similar to saying, "I like animals. What sort? Vertebrates. So I plan to go to the zoo later today where there is a special vertebrates exhibit."

3. But why is *creative nonfiction* so fraught? And why do people react to fiction the way they do? I think one answer will suffice for both questions. We would like reality to be simple; it isn't. That doesn't mean there aren't facts, but instead that proving what we experience is extremely difficult. So, we believe, if we avoid *fiction*, if we avoid the *un*real, then we will live in a real world, obviously real, clearly real, unimpeachably real. This dream, frayed before it was ever fully formed, disintegrates with celerity, and we are left with the creeping dread that not only is reality not simple, it's not even as *real* as we would like. And so any label we stick on that which is supposed to be grounded in the real is just as irksome, just as prickly, just as dubious as our reality, and therefore just as likely to be dismissed by us as inadequate. And we are right to feel this way because fiction is in everything. I argue, this swirl of fiction and nonfiction, of reality and perhaps its opposite, makes the world wonderfully complex, not in a beautiful way, but in a sublime way.

Kitchen Sink Realism

Morning

Christmas morning of my second grade year I sat at the red cloth covered kitchen table eating cinnamon rolls, having just opened all of my presents, the debris of torn paper that used to conceal now ravaged and discarded everywhere, the tree a bit aslant from Charney the dog's own bounding excitement that sent slobber and then boxes and then my family into the air to avoid the rampage, ending with her finally careening into the base of the faux pine, while outside the snow melted, the cold abating for a brief respite before the ice-fingered grip and persistent storms of January and February would coat our world, really it seemed permanently, where we might forget what it all looked like under that blanket of white, but of course we didn't forget, and when the snow would disappear sometime in April we'd be reintroduced to what we already knew. Steve Farkas, my dad, as he would many times in the future when I was grown and out of college and living back at home, as he would when he needed someone to talk to long into the evening (so long it was actually early in the morning) after another session at the bar, as he would when he needed an auditor to listen to his musings, when he needed a sympathetic ear to hear his laments, when he needed a compadre to answer or at least to join him in thinking about his questions, yes my dad leaned against the sink and lit a cigarette as I asked about Santa Claus. Looking at me out of the corner of his eye, his irises almost as dark as his pupils, turning now toward the sink, flicking ashes into the drain, taking in the snow-melt of the backyard, me in the periphery, he said, "You don't still believe in Santa Claus, do you?" And although I'd opened a gift that listed "Santa Claus" as the giver not ten minutes before, and although I hadn't doubted that little tag for one second, I realized my dad was right. I didn't believe in Santa Claus. There was no pain. There was no feeling of loss. I only knew that once I'd believed in Santa Claus, but that time was over.

Evening

Sometime during my junior year of high school, so late at night it was technically early in the morning, I sat at my friend Steve Byrd's bare kitchen table, the both of us having cleared away the pieces to Warhammer Quest, a game where each move reveals a new section of the game board, and we found ourselves, in the semi-dark house lit only by a light shining from above the sink, in one of those conversations people have when they're tired but don't feel like sleeping, even though there's nothing to do, and so to keep things going, to ward off the silence that had descended, that threatened an unwanted terminus, I asked a question about God. Steve, as I had probably never seen him before, the windowless and technology-crammed basement our normal purlieu, hunched over the counter looking out into the darkness of the night or the morning, glanced down at the drain, then turned, the reflection of the light bulb visible on his glasses reminding me of the cartoon signal for an idea, and, eyeing me directly, he said, "You don't still believe in God, do you?" I looked outside and realized that morning wasn't characterized by blaring light any more than evening was characterized by absolute darkness, and although without the electricity pulsing through the carbon filament I wouldn't have been able to see a thing, I knew it was morning, and that I hadn't believed in God for some time.

Time Stands Still When You're Havin' Fun

With a nod to Sam Shepard

We're playing Texas Hold'em.
Again?
Didn't we play that last time?
We did. But next time . . . we'll play something else.
I'm in.
Course you are.
No one folds.
No different than slots. Shovel the chips in and see what happens.
It's just money. They print more every day.
Seven for the flop.
Seven of our best.
It's only seven people at the table!
Everyone checks.
You guys know where I can find a poker game around here?
Next card.
Everyone checks.
You watch, I'll get screwed on the river.
And you'll be out ones of dollars. Guess they'll have to update the richest people list.
River.
A six-dollar bet; a reluctant call.
A pair of threes.
You play that trash?
Another pair of threes.
Pause.
Well, this is some championship poker we've got here, folks.

We're playing...

I've heard poker described as "hours of Boredom punctuated by moments of Terror." Problem is, I've heard soldiers used that line to describe war.

So maybe, maybe it ought to be "hours of Boredom punctuated by moments of..." Well, of what? Apprehension? Doubt? Worriment? Fretfulness? How about excitement? Mild excitement. "Hours of Boredom punctuated by moments of Mild Excitement." Doesn't have the same oomph to it, but what the hell. This ain't war. It's $3–$6.

Yeah, sure, we're talking Texas Hold'em, same as they have on the TV. Though about as similar as Major League Baseball is to a slow-pitch softball game where the players've set up a keg at first base. What you see on TV, that's No Limit, a game based on psychologically manipulating your opponent into thinking, hell, *believing* you've got the best hand, a game where the goddamn cards almost up and disappear, a game that brings us as close as we'll ever get to a psychic competition.

But in $3–$6, your most fearsome foe, once you have the game down pat, ain't Wild Bill Hickok or Nick the Greek or Doyle Brunson. Matter of fact, it ain't a person at all. No, something far more sinister. This desperado is waiting for you at every single poker room in the whole wide world, and if there are poker rooms on other worlds, damned if it ain't there too. Boredom.

Because $3–$6, friends, is a structured betting game, meaning for the first two rounds you can only wager increments of $3 and the last two rounds increments of $6, and you don't get to pick which increment, you gotta follow the order. Unlike No Limit, then, there's precious little psychology, no psychic powers at all, and the cards *always* remain painfully present. To win, you gotta fold and fold and fold and fold, until the odds are in your favor; to win, you can't get depressed when you realize you haven't played a hand in a few hours; to win, you can't let the fact that some bastard so drunk he can't even see his own cards (let alone the shared cards at the center of the table) lucked out. This game, it ain't about taking the pots you ought to take, but about staying away from the hands you shouldn't've played in the first damned place. How do you go about doing that? You have to see the poker world, sure, but you also have to look beyond it. Or Boredom will be victorious, and you, buddy, you'll be broke.

But now why is it when there're so many more horrible things in the world, death, torture, rape, disease, hunger, actual Nazis, physical pain of all sorts, mental pain of all sorts, fear itself, that folks include Boredom in that list of awfulness, when really, all it is, I mean no one's kicking your ass, threatening your family, nuking your future plans, telling you that the problem is you got this condition ain't no one's ever heard of before, no, you're just bored, nothing to do, which, no offense pal, are you kidding me? why is *that* such a problem, so much so that psychiatrists, psychologists, sociologists, scientists of all kinds, even philosophers have written about it, studied it, thought about it, no one more so than Martin Heidegger, that old Nazi, who went on forever and ever about the three stages of Boredom (can you feel the z's creep up on you when you think about sitting through those goddamned long-winded lectures?), who showed us how Boredom is connected to time and meaning, but then, there at the climax, okay, for fuck's sake, lay it on us already . . . but no. He shows us how Boredom finally comes to an end (strangely not by shutting the hell up, but never mind), but not why it's a problem in the first damned place.

Anyway, to pass the time, as we wait for answers to our questions, as we wait for some goddamn cards, which, sad to say, could be quite a while; and the longer the layover lasts, the more it gets to feeling like you're at a bus station and the bus's due, overdue, long overdue, which ain't so surprising at first, a late bus, gonna go out on a limb here and say it's happened before, gonna go further out on that limb and say it'll happen again, gonna blindfold myself and take off at a sprint on this limb to say it'll happen again many, many, many times, no fear at all that I might fall out of this metaphorical tree, hell, it'd be goddamned bewildering if the coach were ready to go at the listed time, could be the harbinger for the end of days, eschatological horseshit from the religious canon be damned, instead, here it is 11:07 on the nose and what in *the* hell are we doing? yeah, rolling out of the station, Hades following, just as confused as the rest of us, almost makes you want to go up, pat the ruler of the underworld on the back and say, Come on, bub, you're the, uh, well, supernatural entity for this here job, been preparing for all eternity, and so, what I want you to do, don't hold back, pal, go out there and really. . . but right now, what luck, the apocalypse ain't upon us on account of the expected lag, so until we get some cards, I've got this story to tell you.

Goes like this:

The Legend of That Guy You Replaced Your Son With

There was a man in the Queen of Hearts Club, up there in Billings, Montana, who went by something or other, no doubt, but I'll call him Herald. And Herald was perfect and upright (not three sheets like some), a guy who feared the bad beat, and generally steered clear of sucker straights . . . *Herald?* Yeah, I know, it ought to be *Harold*, since that's a person, right?, a guy, guy you can drink a beer with, guy you can watch a ballgame with, guy you can turn to and say, I was thinking of reorientating this impromptu shindig we're having in more of a bowling direction, you down?, of course he'd be down, and after you'd gotten the shoes, the ball, the lane, you'd look up and see your new pal'd already filled out the scorecard: H-A-R-O-L-D, and reading his moniker you'd get this warm feeling in part because you'd made a new friend, and ain't that nice?, in part because you're about to do some bowling, which's nice too, but also on account of this thought just entered your noggin that all was right with the world, even though it sure as hell wasn't, not even close, that everything was gonna be okay, though it probably won't be anything like okay, and you know it, but, behold!, thus is the power of that there arrangement of letters: H-A-R-O-L-D.

Herald, on the other hand.

Goddamn.

No one goes by that.

'Cause it's just not a name. . .

Only, who cares?, since it wasn't his name either. Well, probably it wasn't. I mean, I never heard his name. Or, if I did, I don't remember it. . . Lemme tell ya, he *looked* like a Harold, yeah, on account of the fact that everyone at this table looks like a Harold, that's why he was perfect, because everyone at a \$3–\$6 table is old, even the young folks are old, and no one pretends to be anything but, least of all our friend here, and just in case you thought you could pull one over on us, there's a rule, at the Queen of Hearts, in this casino, and in every other poker room in the world, says you can only speak in one language: Cliché. I was sure, if he graced us with his words, they wouldn't actually be his words, they'd be someone else's words, passed down through the generations, so familiar I could join in along with all the other Harolds, like as if we were reciting the lyrics to some ancient song absolutely everyone knows and no one needs to fear.

Oh, but we should've been afraid.

Really afraid.

Because when he finally spoke, in violation of all the natural laws, this man sang his own terrifying song, and I haven't recovered since:

"Our son died. And the guy we replaced him with was eaten by a bear. He just got in the cage with the bear. And the bear ate him."

Quoth Herald.

Maybe a few minutes before, except it seemed like eons at that point, he was just another lousy poker player at the Queen of Hearts. . . Goddamn guy was just another Harold.

After he spoke, well, there'd probably been less commotion if he'd up and turned into a sphinx. . .

Now listen:

In Cincinnati, this was years ago, I was driving a moving truck with side mirrors that stuck out way farther than I was used to, and the telephone poles, for whatever reason, were really close to the road, only I didn't realize any of that at the time, so the crash and the explosion, what caused either of them was a mystery to me, not helped by the fact that everything was suddenly in slow motion, actual slow motion, glass moving through the cabin at a laggardly pace, no hurry, making me think I could pick each and every fragment out of the air, turn it around in my hand a few times, think about it, really get to know it, maybe write the definitive treatise on that piece, plenty of time here, before, almost sadly, remembering back when I was focused on. . . but no, gotta move onto the next one, even in slow motion you don't get all the time you'd want, going from bit to bit this way, until I became an expert (available for various court proceedings) on the shards that happened to be occupying the airspace inside the U-Haul or Penske or Budget furniture hauler I was obviously doing a bad job of piloting, since I'd rammed a side mirror into a telephone pole, which led to my only experience where time actually . . . slowed . . . down.

That is until right after Herald spoke.

See the poker room. Felt tables. Green or red. Some with markings and lines. Some without. Vinyl leaning strips encircle the felt. Red or black. Office chairs with no arms. Or with arms. Brown and blue. Maybe maroon or beige. Chaotic carpet. Emerald and purple. Navy and gold. Orange and yellow. Other colors too. No discernible pattern. The dealer in polyester. Unflattering long-sleeve shirts. Unflattering for all. Rows and rows of chips. House chips. None of them yours. Cocktail waitresses. Clad like strippers. Clad like casual Friday. A man enters. An emissary. From somewhere else. Calling a name. Walking past a distant bank. Of slot machines. Blinking lights. Pulsing lights. Progressive jackpot. Pink neon piping. A name. The name. Of a winner. Moving through an atmosphere of pure oxygen. No. Moving through an atmosphere perfectly controlled. No. Moving through. Passing by. Pit bosses. Dressed like gangsters. Dressed like cheap PIs. Dressed like fast food managers. Calling a winner. Calling an absent winner. Calling the only publicly known loser. For that day. Moving through a too cold expanse. Moving through an overly mannered expanse. Of the indoors.

And on this space, dreams are printed. By those who don't play. Imagine. You can see it. And by those who do. Close your eyes. Don't let yourself get distracted. The story, these dumb bastards don't have a clue. You know what's *really* going on. You know.

But what bothers me is. Is in that slow motion. I . . . I can't picture Herald. This graybeard. Provided he had a beard. Maybe in a hunting ball cap. A fishing ball cap. A golf ball cap. Just can't recall. And. And anytime I think. I think I've almost got him. Time catches up again. And the Harolds erupt with questions:

"If your son was eaten by a bear, why'd you let the bear live?"

"If that guy knew your son had been eaten by that man-eating bear, why'd he get in the cage?"

"Wait a minute. He didn't say his son was eaten by a bear. He just said his son died and that guy was eaten by the bear. You know, after he got in the cage with it."

"Why'd that guy get in the cage with the bear in the first place?"

"Did that guy blame the bear for your son's death?"

"Did *you* blame the bear for your son's death? Did that guy get in the cage because of *you*?"

I was the only one who said, "The guy you replaced your son with?"

Ladies and gentlemen, I argue this very short story has everything: it has tragedy (a parent having to deal with the death of a child), heroism (the man getting in the cage with the bear), implied action (the battle between the man and the bear), gore (the man losing to the bear), if read the right way it has a moral (don't get into cages with bears), if read another way it has comedy ("He just got into the cage with the bear, and the bear ate him, what'd the dumb bastard think was gonna happen?"), but the one thing it doesn't have is an explanation, since Herald, after telling the story, after being bombarded with questions, said nothing to me, said nothing to the other Harolds, and, like nothing'd happened, he went back to playing poker. . .

So there you are. And since the fervor died down pretty quickly, such that like five minutes later no one seemed to care anymore, nor seemed to think anything out of the ordinary had happened, well, sure, after all that, I guess it's only me, by my lonesome, who can tell you about it.

Was in Tuscaloosa, Alabama, at a fancy-pants restaurant when my friend Whitney Holmes, noting the fancy-pants-edness of the general surroundings, put forth her belief that the purveyors of this here fine establishment can likely make an actual cocktail, not one of those mistakes you get at dives and college bars, where they dump various liquors and mixers into a glass until the glass is full (of what, there's no telling), slopping it in your direction, inviting you to lick the rest off the bar if you don't care for their service, but here, yes right here, they should have the real deal (completely contained in a tumbler, even), so that when the waiter came by and inquired as to what liquid refreshment she might want, Ms. Holmes said:

"A Brandy Alexander."

The waiter said: "A what?"

Ms. Holmes again: "A Brandy Alexander."

The waiter: "A what?"

Ms. Holmes, enunciating slowly: "A rum and Coke."

Whitney calls that move The Abort, only it doesn't seem like you're ready to Abort playing poker yet, since you're still staring down our desperado (with his bent cigarette and his rumpled clothes), even if we're getting into more dangerous territory with him, since that actual Nazi Heidegger said the first stage of Boredom, back when we were just wondering when we might get some goddamned cards already, isn't really all that bad, but the second stage, well, sure, there're times when you win some hands, you lose some hands, you go for a long stretch where all you do is fold, followed immediately by a rush lasts so long you can't actually remember the last time you lost, but it don't matter, you still feel like you're on a bus somewhere, and you're motoring toward your destination, but it's taken so damn long, well, you stop believing in that destination, not sure why you wanted to go there in the first place, *what in the hell am I doing*, you ask yourself, *on this goddamn bus?!*, and as you stand at a rest stop you don't need, but which the rules demand (so says the driver), you look around and the world seems to sprawl out forever, the night sky further than that, and time expands so much it makes the world and space appear downright small, even though you get to feeling there's no end to any of it, making you think it's *you* you're bored of, *you* you can't escape from, so for distraction, why not imagine this story I'm about to lay down takes place in front of us, right here in the casino. . .

The Legend of That Guy Who Sat in the Back of the Room

It befell in my undergrad days, when general education requirements were king, and so reigned, that I signed up for a course called Liberal Arts Math, believing that a person like me, who has the gift of gab, who's good with words, but a complete dunce when it comes to numbers, rightly belonged in such a class, and so I hauled my ass over the hills of the Muskingum College campus in New Concord, Ohio (people who live there haven't heard of it either), to the room where we were to meet, finding like-minded folks who looked at figures as if they were so many mystical symbols only magic-men understood (if truly even *they* did), and so together we readied ourselves for the weak sauce version of mathematics we expected, when Santa Claus made his entrance.

And there came a day when Professor Claus, so named by the girl who in front of me sat because he looked like St. Nick, even drinking out of a teeny tiny coffee cup we called his elf mug, decided to instruct us in the sacred rites and peculiarities of Infinite Set Theory, though we were unlikely to understand a goddamned word of it, having not understood a goddamned word of anything else he'd taught us, seeing as how the course actually should've been called Math for Hardcore Mathematicians, instead of what we secretly thought it was called, that being Math for Students Reluctantly Enrolled in a Math Class, and so Dr. Father Christmas told us about Georg Cantor (likely every bit as imaginary as our North Pole dweller, we thought at the time), and how Cantor showed that there wasn't just one kind of infinity, nah, there're lots of 'em, an infinity of infinities, proved by the fact that any two infinite sets might not be equal, even if they are infinite, skepticism rising, a classroom full of dullards prepared to wage mighty war on the increasingly outrageous concepts being espoused, when Kris Kringle said, take for example all the odd numbers and then all the prime numbers, don't matter that each one of those sets goes on forever, the forever that they go on into ain't the same, which, as you might expect, made the students wondrously wroth, everyone saying infinity is infinity, just like five is five, and there passed a period of riotous jack-assery, no one able to control themselves, until Papa Noel, unfazed, finally called us to order, and explained, saying:

"Two infinite sets might not be equal because . . . they both fail to end in different ways."

Now, there's a guy here I haven't told you about yet, a guy who, well, he's *the* guy, the one who makes the telling worthwhile, the hero, as it were, and like any hero, after his adventure was over, you could hear about him on into the future, from people like me, who were there, present and accounted for, from people I knew, who'd gotten the lowdown from yours truly, and later from folks that'd picked it up I don't know how, spinning questionable versions, not sticking to the canon, maybe unfamiliar with it, so much horseshit added might as well've been titled, "The Legend of This Here Horse and Its Prodigious Amount of Shit," but to set the record straight, I'll have you know that this guy who sat in the back of the room, not only sat in the back of the room, but sat off by himself in the back of the room, making it seem like he was somehow really far away, in his own territory, his own land even, an inexplicably cavernous expanse, so when Professor Claus spoke his immortal line, "Two infinite sets might not be equal because . . . they both fail to end in different ways," and that guy, that guy in the back of the room, in response, well, when he flipped his book closed, the sound that book made echoed, yes, it did, it echoed off the walls, the desks, the blackboard, the ceiling, maybe even off of St. Nick's teeny-tiny elf mug, and without thinking, all of us turned around and looked at him.

With his bag, he stood up like he'd been called away on a mission.

He walked, man did he walk, epics could be written about that journey from the back to the front of the room.

He slapped his hand down on Kris Kringle's desk, saying, in a loud voice: "All right!"

With two fingers, he saluted Professor Claus, who, in that moment, was more confused about what was going on than we were about Infinite Set Theory.

And then, that guy who sat in the back of the room, we didn't know it at the time, since we figured he'd just had enough and was headed in the general direction of his mini-fridge which contained the twelve or eighteen beers he aimed to put away, but no, as he walked out the door, we didn't realize he was departing, just like that, never to grace us with his presence again, we didn't realize this singular moment would be etched on our minds because he'd vanish afterwards, we didn't realize, as he walked out the door, that that'd be the last we ever saw of him. The girl in front of me, Professor Claus, some other folks too, they assumed he wasn't just that guy who sat in the back of the room, but that he'd be the once and future guy who sat in the back of the room, yeah, they assumed he'd return. He never did. But we heard stories. Oh, yes, we ... heard ... stories.

❧

"Long ago, but not too long, and far away, but not so far as all that, in a place not unlike this one, but not exactly the same, it is told that some guy who once sat in the back of a room, only let's call him Guy for short, Guy boarded a bus, for where? even he wasn't sure, and rode around the land until every place became no place, until everywhere became nowhere, his journey ending in a field, as if this field were a place people could buy tickets to, as if the bus had a little electronic readout on the front of it that listed Field as its final destination, as if the driver shouted out, 'Field!' lumbered out the door, unloaded the luggage, and then drove off to the garage, and in that field, Guy passed an unknown amount of time, finally interrupted by a couple who had recently lost a son, who, upon seeing this wayward Guy, thought *he* could be their son, for when asked what his name was, he said, 'I don't know,' and when asked where he was from, he said, 'Infinity,' so the couple took him in, and fed him, and clothed him, and put him to work on the ranch, cleaning the stalls, feeding the horses, mending the fences, life proceeding without incident until the day Guy found the caged bear, why the couple had a caged bear, no one's sure, including the ranch owners, and Guy stared inside, only the husband of the couple there to witness it, afraid to speak, afraid to move, until Guy, as if to the bear, said, 'My name is Herald, and soon I will be invincible,' before stepping inside.

"The husband, after he'd seen the horrors, repeated, 'Herald, my name is Herald,' and headed toward town..."

Heidegger, that son of a bitch, says at the worst stage of Boredom, we feel disconnected from any narrative, we feel like we have no identity, we feel like any one thing is just the same as any other thing, and who in the hell could go on like that for long? but then he tells us how we can snap out of it, though I'd say his supposedly hopeful solution is bullshit, since it's actually why we fear Boredom so much, why it's so bothersome, only a Nazi would torture us with these insanely long lectures, with horrible writing full of new words that do more to cloud sense than make it, and then present us with "hope" in the form of something just about everyone is terrified of, since Heidegger claims at the moment everything appears meaningless, meaning reasserts itself by showing us new stories we could live out, new people we could become, in other words Change, Change is our way out of Boredom, so when Guy looked into that there bear cage, he understood either he'd have to accept Change (but who knows what kind of godawful monster he might become?), or he'd have to find a way to cement who he was, and thinking back to his old math class, he saw the infinite open up, understanding he couldn't comprehend it (not a goddamned word), understanding he had no access to it, dwarfed by the vastness, realizing only through physical obliteration could his true self go on, unsullied, so he decided to protect the little bit he had—himself, which reminds me I haven't told the rest of the story...

The Legend of Herald the Harold

"...in town, at a poker room, Herald told his story. And the guy who heard that story went on to tell it to someone else, who went on to tell it to someone else, who went on to tell it to someone else, each and every one of them taking on the name Herald, transforming into Herald, compelled to go on to some other public place and tell the story again, the mantle and the mission passing to the next person, the story perhaps taking on other true or fictional additions along the way, altered slightly each time, much as former Heralds are left changed forever, nothing like what they used to be. And if you're wondering how you can avoid meeting Herald, how you can continue on with your own life as it is, well, there's no one place he might be, since he could be anywhere; you'll never see him coming, since he looks like everyone, no one. So, I'm afraid all you can do is hope you never run into him."

Unless, that is, you already have.

The cards've been dealt, and before I even look at 'em, I know the way Boredom'll win this time, seeing as how, without a doubt, my hand'll be mediocre, should just throw it the hell away. But I won't throw it away. I'll figure out some goddamned reason why it's okay to stay in, forking over my $3, the bet immediately raised by the next bastard in line, meaning I'll have another chance to get out, but hey, I've come this far, and anyway, that jerk who raised probably doesn't have anything, and then on the flop, Godfrey Daniel! I'll have top pair, though my kicker won't be so good, and there'll be two cards to a flush and two to a straight, neither of which'll be available to me, the turn giving me two pair, though now there'll be three cards to a flush and three to a straight, the river bringing a fourth card to that flush, the hand ending with yours truly in second place, old pal Boredom sitting next to me in a wrinkled suit with tie undone, hair sticking up like he just rolled outta bed, smoking a bent cigarette, patting me on the back, quipping:

"Andy, you should go tell the pit boss you finished in second place, you really should. Because, for folks like you, yeah, *for folks like you* he has a blue ribbon says, 'Winner of Second Place,' right on it waiting back there behind the desk. He's been saving that prize; he *wants* to give it to someone. And, pal, you know what you should do, oh, if only you would, once you've accepted your award: *put that ribbon on.* And, buddy, after you've accepted your award, this would be epic, as a favor just to me: *wear that ribbon always.* Then, that'll be you, forever: the Winner of Second Place."

But it's been so long, so long, what can I do to stop this . . . ?

We're playing Texas Hold'em.

Again?

Didn't we play that last time?

We did. But next time . . . we'll play something else.

The dealer's flung cards to each of the players, none of whose names I know, not even mine. Boredom, with his bent cigarette, looks on, mildly interested, already pointing to where I should wear the ribbon. He takes a drag and my hand's predictably mediocre. But I can get away with playing trash just this once, right? I might even win. It happens for the Harolds all the time. The Harolds who stay forever the same wherever I go.

I reach for my chips. Three chips, that's all. I can feel them in my hand. I can see them moving forward. Who knows what I'd become if I fold again? But I look at Boredom, already holding the Second Place ribbon. . .

And then I say: *Our son died.*

I let the chips stay in their stacks.

And the guy we replaced him with was eaten by a bear.

I toss my cards into the center; Boredom drops his veneer, seems genuinely surprised.

He just got in the cage with the bear.

Later, I'll stand up, adjust the ball cap that obscures my monstrous features, pad away blending in with the crowd. You won't remember me.

And the bear ate him.

On Drinking the Kool-Aid in a Coffeehouse

Walk into any coffeehouse and who will be there? Well, I can already hear someone strumming on an acoustic guitar, knowing full well the musician is completely convinced they're going to make it, regardless of the fact that this is the only venue they've ever played in, regardless of the fact that their twenties are far behind them, regardless of the fact that their set list is entirely composed of cover songs; I can see the students who are going to change the world with their ever-shifting majors sitting next to the graduate students who have absolutely no plan of ever completing their degrees; if you're like me, you're happy to wave at those who have one foot firmly planted in their role playing game worlds, while the other foot is tentatively, one might say gingerly, tapping the real world because it feels like you're hailing an alternate dimension; there are the artistes or authors who talk incessantly about their nonexistent work, haranguing those who have seemingly slapped together the paintings hanging from the walls on their way to get more coffee; there are the hyper-serious pseudo-intellectuals who argue by misquoting philosophers, theorists, thinkers who may not exist anyway, or by creating their own incomprehensible concepts they'll forget themselves directly; there are people playing chess who barely know how each piece moves, but who are convinced they're Bobby Fischer (without the anti-Semitism); there are the aging hippies who perhaps sell marijuana to those working hard to look like potheads, though the ostensible potheads may not smoke at all; and there are people wearing their obscure or outdated politics or religion or mysticism or ufology right on their clothes.

Don't get me wrong. Anytime I go into a coffeehouse, I am happy to see these folks. And I have no problem with people finding and accepting types that feel comfortable to them as long as they remain conscious of the fact that they're playing a role. But I must stop right there. The problem with my catalogue is that the entrees are types bordering on the cliché.

"What's wrong with that?" you might say.

I'm so glad you asked. In my experience, no one thinks of themselves as a cliché. When pressed, we might admit that other people willfully and joyously embrace clichés in speech and in action, but those poor bastards are lazy, weak, or just plain dumb. No intelligent person would allow themselves to become a static character in real life; everyone who's willing to put forth a little effort would choose to be dynamic.

But that's not true.

For example:

Late one Kent, Ohio evening in the middle aughts, I descended (literally, since you had to walk downstairs once you entered) into this coffeehouse milieu. For no reason I could discern, lacking any reference to Alcatraz, the place was called The Rock. But I was happy to be there, not only because I was surrounded by the entertaining types I felt I knew, but because of the time: I'd always wanted coffeehouses to stay open on bar hours and The Rock obliged. The reason for my constant desire: sure, sometimes the pub is the right place, but other times I want to be out late without drinking alcohol (seeing as I'm a night owl). Please notice, though, that I said "coffeehouse," not to be confused with diners (also called greasy spoons, also, confusingly, called coffee shops) which frequently stay open twenty-four hours. A coffeehouse is a very different place with a very different vibe.

That evening, I was prepared to do something I don't actually do that often: I was planning on writing in public. The reason I don't normally do this is because I can't write very well when there's music playing (the acoustic strumming continues on), nor can I write very well when there are people talking around me. Consequently, I usually read in coffeehouses, though I admit the music and talking slow me down there too.

No matter, on that night I was going to write. In public. Meaning I was already going to engage in a clichéd and even self-defeating activity. If that were all, however, there'd be no point to this essay. But that was not all.

Walking through the brick-walled interior decorated by the aforementioned "art" (phenomenally overpriced, natch), past the grungy couches and lounge chairs (I've often thought if you placed a brand new piece of furniture in a coffeehouse, as soon as it touched the floor, it'd look well worn, and thank goodness for that), around a group of late teenagers/early twentysomethings (one of them wearing a red Hammer and Sickle track jacket) who were embroiled in a discussion about something metaphysical or mystical, up to the bar (sometimes the ordering area looks like a counter, this one a bar) over which a blackboard listed all of the drinks and prices in various colors of chalk. Since this particular establishment was definitely in the tradition of those where it seemed like someone's parents thought they could get their goddamn kids out of the house if they and their friends ran a business, I knew not to get anything more complicated than drip (Americanos, cappuccinos, etc.—some other time).

Only, I didn't get drip coffee.

Because, strangely, off by itself on the chalkboard was this: "And Also Kool-Aid."

Although I enjoy nostalgia, I've found I don't need quite so much of it as others. For instance, whereas I liked the candies Skittles and Spree when I was a kid, I've found my adult form never needs to eat them again. The same goes for ramen noodles. The same goes for macaroni and cheese (and "fancy" macaroni and cheese found at hipster restaurants gets nothing but an eye-roll from me).

But for some reason, on this occasion, surrounded by coffeehouse types at about 11:00 p.m., I decided, who cares if I'm thirty, I'm gonna have some Kool-Aid. And as if my scruffy barista knew that this moment should be played for maximum nostalgia, he pulled out a bright-green plastic pitcher with one of those white rotating tops and poured my drink into a translucent red plastic cup, the kind Chuck E. Cheese's, Pizza Hut, and my own family used to have.

Unlike the other drinks, Kool-Aid didn't have a listed price, so I was told it was free ("Hey, man, it's just Kool-Aid!"). I gave the guy a dollar tip, walked back through the group of kids who were all looking at me now (likely because I was the only customer who wasn't a friend of theirs), found a booth, pulled my laptop and my notebook out of my bag, choked down some purple-tasting sugar water, and started working.

An aside:

I am an atheist and have been one since high school. For the brief period of time I was part of a religion, I was Catholic. I do not consider myself a "lapsed Catholic," as some do. At most, I would say I'm an ex-Catholic (and I won't be rekindling the relationship ever). Remarkably, unlike other Christian sects, Catholics are not encouraged to evangelize. There is something to the belief that Catholics look at other Christians and wonder why you would choose to go to Hell when you're more or less on the "right" path. The baseball manager Jim Leyland once said he'd never delivered a pep talk because if millions of dollars and thousands of adoring fans weren't good enough, what could he say to make his players play any better? Catholics think similarly: if you don't follow this religion, you're going to Hell. What else would you need?

Perhaps the only remaining vestige of Catholicism left in me, then, is this confusion about evangelism which, personally, extends into sales. I absolutely can't stand having anyone sell me anything. I once walked into a store that specialized in a product I'd been using for twenty years, then walked right back out empty-handed because someone tried to sell me what I already knew I wanted. The next day I returned, made a beeline for the item, took it to the cash register, said, "I'll take this and nothing else," and the transaction ended.

Conclusion of aside.

For a while, in the coffeehouse, I was exactly where I wanted to be. Slowly, however, I became aware of something, something I didn't expect, a repeated word, a name, actually. I heard it quite a lot in the conversations happening around me, I heard it from the acoustic guitar playing singer. Then, scanning the room, I noticed a duplicated image, appearing far more than I would've guessed. And that's when my coffeehouse began to melt away.

"Upon this rock I will build my church. . ." Oh. That rock.

Well, goddamnit.

The repeated name was, of course, Jesus. The repeated image was, of course, a cross. As I saw my surroundings more clearly, I noticed a particular church was even being advertised alongside the Christian art on the walls. I then looked at my cup of Kool-Aid. I then looked at my cup of *free* Kool-Aid, which I had drank actually, though not metaphorically. I suppose I could say the scales fell from my eyes, but the experience was not a positive one. Instead, I was annoyed. Not that such a place existed, but because I'd allowed my over-excitement for a coffeehouse that stayed open on bar hours to deliver me to a place I'd rather avoid: an auxiliary for an evangelical chapel.

When I looked up at the kids who were hanging out at The Rock, I already knew they were on their way over to me. And I knew what their goal was: they were going to try to sell me something I very much did not want. I wondered if the Soviet Union would help, having been an atheistic empire, but inexplicably the red Hammer and Sickle track jacket led the phalanx approaching my booth.

This is what I should've done:

Before they said anything, I should've stood up and told them I'd made a mistake, that I thought this was an unaffiliated coffeehouse, that I am an atheist who isn't the least bit interested in joining any religion whatsoever. If it seemed like they wanted to hear a bit more from me, I would've added that whereas my atheistic/absurdist view of the universe is right for me, I agree with Albert Camus that it isn't right for everyone, meaning I was fine with their beliefs, as long as they left me alone with my thoughts. I should've then thanked them for their Kool-Aid, packed up my stuff, and left.

The reason I ought to have taken this hypothetical course of action is because, as a teacher, I don't actually care what other people believe, as long as they're respectful of others. I want my students to become better writers, yes. But what they happen to write about is up to them. And whereas I teach absurdist literature and cult movies that undermine much of mainstream ideology, I remind the class they don't have to agree with the artists in question, they just have to understand what the writers or filmmakers are doing. Anyway, my students mostly think of these works as "weird," until we discuss them, then the students think of these works as "kinda weird." My general approach to life, then, is if you ask me what I think, I'll tell you, and if you disagree with me, that's fine. On the other hand, if I ask you what you think, I'll listen, and if I don't agree with you, that's also fine. If I would've delivered the above speech, I would've gotten my views across and I would've been myself.

Instead, this is what happened:

As the phalanx approached, I figured I knew what was coming, though I didn't want it to. But, luckily (or so I thought at the time), the Soviet Union made a blunder by asking me what I was working on.

I have the following degrees: a bachelor's, two masters', and a PhD. At every stage, I had to defend either a thesis or a dissertation, and these theses and this dissertation were all made up of my fiction writing. In order to defend them, I had to answer questions posed to me by a committee. In the coffeehouse, I thought at the time, another committee stood before me. My tactic at every defense was the same: I aimed to take so long answering any question that no one would want to ask me another. I did this because, honestly, I'm not the most confident person, so I figured the more time I took, the less likely the committee could stump me. Granted, the committees still asked more questions, and I always did well at the defenses, but in my mind it's because I gobbled up so much time they never got to the hard ones. And so I looked at the Hammer and Sickle, the other assorted members of the phalanx, I restated their inquiry, and then I delivered my response.

By the time I finished telling them about the novel I was working on (which I ended up abandoning anyway), about the books I read to research for the novel, about the other works I perused to help with the style of the novel, about the artistic theories and movements that influenced me, about the artistic theories and movements I was opposed to (illustrating the ways, by using copious examples, I was working against those theories and movements), about how this novel was similar to, but also different from the two collections of short fiction I'd already written (I made sure to tell them the titles: *Self-Titled Debut* and *Sunsphere*), and even about how I'd gotten into writing in the first place, only a deflated version of the Soviet Union remained, the Hammer and Sickle having lost their evangelical spirit, the phalanx having dispersed.

Then there was a long pause . . .

Until, finally, even perfunctorily, the Soviet Union said:

"So, have you heard about Jesus?"

I nodded.

"I have," I said.

There was another long pause.

"Okay." Then the Soviet Union looked at the floor, did an about face, and walked off.

I felt victorious, but I was not. And I wasn't victorious because I wasn't myself. Instead, in a desperate attempt to defend a fantasy, a coffeehouse that stays open on bar hours, I'd become the pretentious asshole who goes on and on and on about what he's doing, the jerk who refuses to shut up and let someone else speak, the know-it-all who no one listens to, or who, more correctly, people rarely listen to, except at certain times (the pretentious asshole's line: "I'm so glad you asked"), when the other denizens of the caffeine cave want to be awed by the sheer wall of verbiage he's able to construct between himself and everyone else. Yes, even though I'd spent my life in creative and intellectual pursuits, even though I most certainly should've known better, meaning others who should know better could fall into the same trap, sitting there, plastic cup in hand, I reified my dream by joyously turning myself into a generic type you'd expect to find in a coffeehouse. I drank the Kool-Aid. I became a cliché.

Still Life with Alarm Clocks

f you close your eyes, you can see the motel room. You can. It's right there. Right there in front of you. It's yours. At least for the night. You can lie down and . . .
Oh, sure, in the moment, with the Highway Hypnosis, the road seems to go on forever. For Andrew Everett Farkas. Who's called Andy. Who thinks of himself as Andy. And so, for Andy, with a bad case of White Line Fever, the road appears to go on forever. But soon enough, oh soon enough, he'll exit (at long last!) the highway, yes, it can be done, he'll exit the highway, he'll pay at the desk, having made no reservations (meaning, even now, Andy doesn't know this room, this room you can see, is to be his), he'll limp through the door, take a shower, collapse on the bed, watch some TV, and then, oh then, yes then, he'll go to sleep.

Later, he'll be awakened by the alarm clock.
At between 3:00 and 4:00 a.m..
Though he didn't set the alarm clock.
There being no reason to wake up at such a strange hour.

Four times this has happened to Andy. The alarm clock. Not set by him. 3:00– 4:00 a.m.. In anonymous motel rooms. In motel rooms he did not reserve beforehand. Sitting in the pre-dawn darkness, the grating sound setting his teeth on edge, Andy will wonder how this came to be, how this could happen, why, why, feeling surrounded by answers, the air vibrating with them, until he fumbles around, turns on a light, shuts the racket off and . . .

For now, the room is vacant—calm—ready to let. Lacking any signs of the soon-to-be occupant. Who is still out on the road anyway. Wondering where he is. Wondering if the lane markings are beginning to bend in on themselves. Wondering if this trip will ever end. He doesn't know yet—it will. But not with the relief he expects. Instead, when he unlocks the door, he won't recognize that sharp click as the sound of inevitability, as the harbinger for a whole new set of perhaps inexplicable circumstances. Instead, Andy, sweaty, discombobulated, a bit achy, thankful he's no longer on the road, innocent of that which is to come, will merely stumble blearily inside.

Inside of the motel room.
Just close your eyes.
You can see it.
Like it's right there in front of you.

On a nightstand in between two double beds, next to a slip that says which numbers correspond to which TV stations, next to menus and contact information for lousy delivery joints, next to a landline telephone with a card over the keypad that instructs you how to ring the front desk and how to dial out, amidst all of this sits the alarm clock. Silent. For now. For now. But, *yeah baby*, in a few minutes, *this one's a fuckin' classic*, in just a few minutes, been waitin' all goddamn night has Carruther (the name Andy's attributed to him), even, what?, laid off the last few Bud Lights so he didn't pass the hell out because *this* can't be missed, *hell no!*, because what's gonna happen, right at 3:14 a.m., the alarm clock, *oh my fuckin' Gawd!*, will engorge and ejaculate its sound again and again and again, a sonic facial, sending whatever asshole happens to be sleeping in that room into the air, thinking it must be time to get up, thinking he must've set the motherfucker (why else would it be shooting off the way it is?), thinking about where he needs to be, whether he's gonna be late or if he has time to make some shitty coffee from the maker over there on top of the mini-fridge, shovel some desiccated nondairy creamer into the swill to give it that wet sand texture to really start the day off right, *yeah buddy!*, until, and really Carruther wishes he could be there for this part (or so Andy assumes), the part when that sad bastard in the room looks at the time and sees ain't nowhere he's gotta be, ain't nothing he's gotta do, since it's three in the goddamned morning! *Wow! Just fuckin' wow, man.*

This ain't Carruther's first rodeo either. Ever since, when was it?, that rank ass flophouse didn't even have dirty movies for fuck's sake, almost a goddamned tragedy, but on that fateful day, and this made it all worthwhile, after downing a six-pack of Coronitas (*who in the Sam Hell sells half-sized beers?!*), his eyes fell on the alarm clock and a spark of genius, abso-*fucking*-lutely, *genius* is the right word, *evil genius?*, fine, best kind, Carruther realized (or so Andy figures) what he could do. Initially, he thought about two in the morning, but some rat bastard night owl (like Andy) might crash here, and then where in the name of piss would he be? Shit outta luck's where. That's when he came up with 3:00 and 4:00 a.m., veering toward the in-between times for whatever diabolical reason. And as he set the inaugural alarm, he was moved by the moment. Moved. Even took off his cheap mesh baseball cap (if he happened to be wearing one) and put it over his heart to properly observe the depths of jackassery he had finally—sunk to? Nah. The depths of jackassery he had finally, successfully achieved. Should be a motherfuckin' holiday.

Over the years, as Andy sees it, Carruther's continued on. And goddamn, you know what?, it's never gotten old. Not even a little bit. Sure, the first time's always the best, but you don't stop jerkin' off just because the first time's behind you, do ya? Hell no! Actually, setting these alarm clocks, it's added so much to Carruther's life, he's not sure how he lived before. Can you even call that *living*? I mean, can you . . . ? There is one question Carruther has, though he knows it'll likely never be answered, but if it could, *oh baby!*, if it could, he could die right there on the spot happier than any other son of a bitch who ever lived: "Have I ever punked the same person twice or even more than twice?" It is his heart's greatest wish. If only Carruther could meet Andy, he'd learn that he hadn't labored in vain.

"Often in actual life, and not infrequently in the myths and popular tales, we encounter the dull case of the call [to adventure] unanswered," says Joseph Campbell in *The Hero with a Thousand Faces* (1949). And, indeed, three times Andy has, seemingly, ignored the call. But in a few minutes, as he lies asleep on the room's king-sized bed, there will be a fourth. Now, you might say, when the alarm goes off, that Andy could ring the front desk and bawl out the night clerk, who would, in turn, offer not only to refund Andy's money, but also send up some "company," which in itself could lead to the expected sex, or melodrama (when the woman admits this is her first night on the job, a job she has only taken because of extremely unfortunate circumstances, driving Andy to do whatever he can to help her out of this situation), or intrigue (when the woman reveals something revelatory that points to a potential plot, one that's perhaps dubious in nature to anyone save Andy, the woman having skillfully recruited Andy through her passionate telling, her desperate telling, her alluring telling of her, granted, questionable story, the scenario ultimately taking our two characters through a series of episodes escalating in tension, until we reach the shocking climax where . . . something or other happens), or confusion (when the "company" turns out to be an octogenarian who, through a befuddling collection of half-told, quarter-told, barely told, and re- told tales that make us think more of con men rather than dementia, we learn that the elderly man was in a, sure, unspecified war, has been missing and presumed dead from the end of that persistently ill-defined conflict, has only reached the country in the past year, wondering if he can bring himself to re- turn to the land of his birth, penniless as he is, but maybe if you, was it *Andy?*, could chauffer me, could pretend to be my compatriot—forty year age gap not bothering him at all—perhaps the folks back home would be more likely to accept my appearance at this late date).

On the other hand, Andy could yank the alarm clock out of the wall, storm down to the lobby, demand to know why in the world . . . but before he can finish, he'll be interrupted by an in-progress robbery (an action story), a drug deal in the process of going wrong (a suspense story), a parent who's been evicted and needs a place to put the kids up for the night (a sob story), a trippy clown convention that has either gotten lost (a comedic story), or arrived here for inexplicable reasons (an artsy story), or that claims to have gotten lost, but as the plot continues to unfold their (the clowns') objectives grow in oddity until the expected corpses start showing up (a horror story), and all because Andy got his lazy ass out of bed (since it's unlikely he'd be able to catch any- more z's anyway), instead of pretending to sleep after shutting the racket off. . . which, as it turns out, is what he *actually* does.

Is Andy, therefore, *dull*, as Joseph Campbell would have it? Because he has brought all of these potential stories to a screaming halt, it might seem so, but he is not. For, as is the case in motels across the country, the heating/air con- ditioning unit can only be dialed to one of two settings: too hot or too cold. On this occasion, Andy has chosen too hot, and thus sleeps on the top cover, which all of his germophobe friends live in terror of, since that blanket is sup- posedly teeming with bacteria, bacilli, pathogens, viruses, and generally icky microorganisms that would just love to get their hooks into a person. Andy, our hero, is undaunted. And in a few moments, when he snorts awake thanks to the alarm clock and then shuts it off, dwell not on the tales we will never get to tell, but instead on *The Saga of Andy, Defier of Motel Blanket Microbes.* Let it be sung for eons to come!

Sitting on the likely stained, always uncomfortable lounge-style chair in the room, drinking a Rainier, wondering what that smell is (before driving this thought from his mind forever), watching sports highlights on ESPN or movies on HBO (rarely having either channel at home), holding the remote, since Andy mostly stays in cheap motels, it might seem like he's a *mostly* insignificant guy, or at least no more significant than any other average human. But this is not the case. After all, someone must be setting the alarm clocks. Since someone is setting the alarm clocks, for at least one person, Andy is extraordinary, worthy of covert harassment the way an antagonist would be. Having explained to his classes that *Dr. Farkas* is obviously not a hero's name, our villain does not disagree with this assessment. And yet who is obsessed over more than an enemy? No one. So, it is proven that Dr. Farkas is not only important, but maximally so . . . for at least one person.

Except that *one* person is not enough. If Dr. Farkas were more methodical, if, when he took his road trips, he planned ahead and reserved a room in a specific motel, then one person would be enough. Instead, like a mad scientist of the highway, he stops wherever and whenever the feeling grabs him. The person, or actually the *people* who find Dr. Farkas to be maximally important cannot, therefore, be called *stalkers*, since *stalker* implies following. Instead, they must precede him, they must predict which motel he will stop at, they must augur which room he will end up in, they must even deactivate all of the erroneous alarms they've set (since Dr. Farkas has not met anyone else who's had *his* experience). Mentally, Dr. Farkas, when he starts his car at the beginning of a journey, sees this squad, no, this group, no, this hoard fan out along his prospective path, friendly rivalries having formed, veterans taking rookies under their collective wings, bets being laid with bookies who've glommed onto this massive strike force, money getting exchanged for tips on sure things that are anything but certain, true believers declaring systems that aren't exactly systematic, all in the name of flicking a switch in the right room, the room where the dastardly Dr. Farkas will attempt to rest.

As haunting symphonic music fills this motel lair, from his vile throne, hand sitting atop the controls, Dr. Farkas watches as an army fans out on the screen, a confident army, an army unaware of what they're walking into. Interesting that there are so many buttons on this remote—buttons everyone is familiar with, buttons few are familiar with. *Very few*. Our villain holds the clicker aloft, having known full well who was pestering him all this time; he's merely been waiting for the right moment. Finger poised above what could be the explosive plunger, that which could thwart his petty adversaries forever, he looks at his beverage and remembers the barkeep who told him it's pronounced *Ron-yay*. The fiend pauses . . . and then pushes the big red OFF button. Let them have their fun a little longer. They really are quite adorable . . . in a pathetic sort of way. And anyhow, sometime soon, Dr. Farkas will make them pay. Oh, he'll make them all pay. Just not yet, he thinks, patting the remote. Not yet.

彩

Right as he shuts the shower off, Andy thinks he hears an odd noise coming from the main room. Was it the front door? The heater/air conditioner? The TV? Someone in an adjoining room? He's not sure. Nor is he sure if his mind is playing tricks on him. Maybe there was no strange sound. Maybe there was and is nothing. When Andy was younger, he was highly susceptible to para-lyzing fear, a sensation that could be activated by even a slightly creepy com-mercial about UFOs, a sensation that would not leave sometimes for days. In junior high, however, he forced himself to watch a series of horror films (*A Nightmare on Elm Street* 1–6) by himself until he purged this irrational response. Once in a while, though, Andy's mind can still be sent reeling by clicks, or creaks, or taps, or the like. Still standing in the tub, Andy wonders if he should turn the faucet back on, as if the potential intruder might let his, her, or even *its* guard down thanks to the water's roar.

Wait a minute: *It*?

What could *It* be?

Now holding the doorknob, Andy thinks about the fact that motel rooms resemble living spaces that humans occupy, yes, *resemble*, but they're not quite right. More like an approximation. The version that'd appear in an anthro-pological museum far in the future. Or, the version that'd appear on another planet explaining, to the best of the extraterrestrials' ability, how the race *Homo sapiens* happens to live.

Slowly opening the door, what waits for Andy on the other side? Little green men? Tall grays with large, black eyes? A human-like species with a high creep factor (thanks to the Uncanny Valley effect) that you just know, evi-dence unnecessary, will transport you to their flying saucers, freeze you, and ship you back to their home planet for food like the Visitors in *V* (1983) or the Kanamits from *The Twilight Zone*'s "To Serve Man" (1962)? Is that what's waiting on the other side of the door? Should Andy maybe rip the towel bar or the shower curtain rod off the wall to use as a weapon? Or are they already in his mind, making resistance futile? There's nothing wrong here. Everything is perfectly fine. Come with us. On our planet there's even a game like baseball we're sure you'll love . . .

Is there anything Andy can do?

Well, no.

Because the only thing on the other side of the door is a curious little cubby for the sink. Andy has often wondered why motel sinks aren't in the bathroom, since that's the normal setting in houses and apartments across the country. Of course, the answer could be that there are also washbasins elsewhere (kitchens, laundry rooms, garages, etc.), so in this approximation of a human living space, the sink is *near* the lavatory, but not *in* it. Andy almost thinks he can hear the alien explaining to its fellow extraterrestrials the use of the spigot and bowl, its usual placement . . .

Was there another sound?

Rapidly drying himself off, throwing on the shorts and T-shirt he intends to sleep in (if there is to be any sleep tonight, if there ever is to be any sleep . . . again), Andy darts into the main room, frantically looking around, as if the intruders were somehow able to hide no matter how fast he moves his eyes, everything suspicious, the mini-fridge that never works right (either it's frozen-over or warm), the iron (who's ironing clothes in a roadside motel?!), the desk with pens and stationery (who's conducting business or writing vacation-like postcards in a roadside motel?!), the curtains . . .

As is normal, the curtains are drawn. There are occasional sounds from outside (cars, doors, rolling bag wheels, people), but nothing unusual. Right? Standing stock-still directly outside of the little hallway that leads to the sink room that leads to the bathroom, wary of everything (who's ever seen hangers like that?!), do the noises sound maybe too, how should we say it, regularized? Like an ambient background generator is at work? What about that light coming in from between the curtains, the curtains that can never be closed all the way for *some* reason? Are the curtains like that because the aliens need to see in? Is it because they've designed this habitat so they can . . . watch?

Is Andy certain if he threw open the front door that he'd see a motel near the expressway? Or would he see a world he's never laid eyes on before? Would the front door even open if he turned the knob? Or is this where he lives now because he agreed (though he doesn't remember it) to follow those nice people (not the right word, as it turns out) to the ship?

Andy decides that, after a day of driving, he's just tired. His imagination is getting the better of him. There's no need to look outside. There's no need to wonder about the placement of the sink. There's no need to worry about the mini-fridge he isn't going to use anyway. The only thing needful is sleep.

Climbing into bed, Andy shuts off the lights using the singular switch that operates two lamps (one click ignites the left, another click, the right, a third, both, then darkness). Immediately thinking better of it (who in the world has lamps like this?!), he quickly turns both lights back on, walks over to the mini-hallway, turns on *that* light (since it won't shine directly in Andy's face while he's sleeping), shuts the bedside lamps off once again before passing out.

One thing the aliens have noticed about humans is that they regularly set and are awakened by alarm clocks (perhaps compensating for some evolutionary flaw), though the wake up times, to the watchers, still appear arbitrary. Furthermore, the aliens have noticed that whereas humans often use alarm clocks, sometimes they don't. On the occasions when they don't, it is frequently because they forgot. Still approximating, the aliens are unsure of when Andy wants to wake up. They are certain, however, that some time is better than no time.

Somewhere, out there on the road, maybe heading from Knoxville or Tuscaloosa or Chicago or Billings or Lawrence to Northeast Ohio (the place he still calls home), Andy fantasizes, as he gets hit by a wave of exhaustion that tells him he must pull off soon, a normal occurrence even after a brief period of cruising along, as normal as the waves of elation that tell him he could drive to the moon if it were physically possible, well Andy fantasizes about the end of the day, about the cheap beer he can sip on, about the chair he can recline on, the TV he can veg on, the pizza he can munch on, the bed he can (finally) sleep on, the motel room where he can just be, rather than going through the perpetual cycle of soaring elation and crushing boredom, only when he does, when he dreams of that motel room, he can't help but think about the alarm clock, about the four times (maybe soon to be five in the near future), realizing he doesn't know where each instance took place, simultaneously believing he's had the experience in every motel room he's ever stayed in and none of

the motel rooms he's stayed in, though obviously neither of those options is possible, making him wonder why something so memorable is so difficult to recall, perhaps making it even more likely that it'll happen again, meaning what he should probably do is remember to check the goddamned clock when he gets to the motor lodge where he'll finally stop.

Only the chances of that happening are nil. Nil, because before he stops there will be elation. Nil, because before he stops there will be boredom. Nil, because before he stops there will be four million other memories, thoughts, waking nightmares, dreams. But still, when it happens again, and it will, he'll say, "Next time, oh next time, I will remember."

❧

Someone must have been telling lies about Andy F., for without having done anything wrong he was arrested in his motel room one fine morning. Well, although technically morning, F. thinks while sitting up in the twin bed, it still looks like night. And he hasn't been arrested in the police, handcuffs, headquarters, jail fashion. No, more like F. has been arrested from sleep by the blaring of the clock. As for having done nothing wrong, F. is, of course, guilty of the usual human misdeeds and errors, but none of the major ones. He certainly hasn't done anything that would lead a person to exact this bizarre form of retribution on him, setting motor lodge alarms to go off at ungodly hours. And so, as he turns to the clock in the darkness wondering what in the world is going on, someone must have been telling lies about Andy F.

Except that *someone* has done no such thing.

Switching on the light in this awkward space (two small bedrooms connected by a door, and a second door in the unused bedroom leading to the bathroom, everything paneled like a 1970s basement), F. finds these feelings of victimization to be just as ridiculous as the overabundance of guilt often connected to Catholicism and Judaism, but which others also appear to feel. He believes people hold onto such ideas because they offer *satisfying* (not to be mistaken with *true*) explanations for why things happen, when the actual explanation in most situations is likely quite boring. Example: while dusting, the cleaning staff, having to move quickly, inadvertently set the alarm, and F. has, curse the luck, stayed in four rooms where this accident has occurred. The End.

If F. kept this to himself, maybe it would be *the end*. But, for argument's sake, let's say that F. decides to complain (certainly it wouldn't take long to make sure the alarm isn't set, certainly that wouldn't increase the onus on the cleaning staff too much). And so, in this hypothetical, he leaves his room wearing his shorts and T-shirt, moves through the labyrinth of walkways and staircases that lead to more walkways and more staircases which give out on a dizzying array of buildings and rooms connected by walkways and staircases, until he finally, somehow, finds himself at reception (the structure itself a rather dramatic A-frame) and then inside at the front desk, where there is, unsurprisingly, no one. F. presses what looks like a doorbell set into the counter. And waits. And waits. And waits some more. And looks over at the nook where the continental breakfast is served, a continent, as it turns out, where everything has gone stale, a landmass made up of the unchewable, a vast expanse of the indigestible. Pressing the doorbell again, F. can feel himself going stale, as if he were a pulverized pile of inedible Froot Loops dust, prepared to be buffeted mindlessly and absurdly by the winds like snow across Antarctica.

"Is there a problem, sir?" the clerk might say, after finally and mysteriously materializing.

"I'm afraid there is. I was sleeping peacefully when the alarm clock woke me up."

"Did you set the alarm clock, sir?"

"Did I *set* the alarm clock? It's 3:30 in the morning."

"I don't know what your . . . *habits* are, sir."

"My *habits*? What're you getting at?"

"I am not . . . *getting* at anything, sir."

"Just the way you said *habits* made it sound like you thought I'd . . ."

"I didn't say . . . *habits* in any particular way, sir. If you are feeling . . ."

"Never mind what I'm feeling. How could you let this happen? Is it so hard to . . . ?"

"I haven't allowed anything to happen, sir."

"I guess you're fine with errantly set alarm clocks waking people up at ungodly hours all the time, huh?"

"This is the first I've heard of it, sir."

"Well, it's not the first time it's happened to me!"

"Here, sir?"

"Not here, elsewhere."

"*Oh*," he draws (or might draw) this out quite a bit. "I see, sir."

"What?"

"This happens to *you*. All. The. Time."

"No! Not *all the time*. Sometimes, sure . . ."

"I am sorry, sir."

"Are you apologizing for . . . ?"

"I am sorry this has happened to *you*. Again. Whatever you have done to bring this . . ."

"I haven't done . . ."

"Of course not, sir."

"I mean, right? I haven't done anything to deserve this . . . have I?"

Beat.

"I don't know your . . . *habits* . . . sir."

Looking at the clock, F. decides it'd be best not to complain. In fact, he decides it'd be best to not talk about this, to *never* talk about this . . . again. He could only imagine what they'd think, what they'd do. So, yes, on this topic, silence . . . But then maybe they already know, maybe they've already come to the conclusion that this is deserved, or even that this chastisement lacks the necessary severity, that a greater punishment is needed, that even the agents they have sent are inadequate to exact the . . . Only, how could he tell if they know, how could he know that they know . . . ? F. thinks of the labyrinth of walkways and staircases and dreams of escape. But there is none. His only hope is to pretend that nothing's happened (though it has); his only hope is to act as if they don't know (though they might). He must bear his burden privately, even if it tears him apart; he must operate with the knowledge that if his secret ever got out, the shame of it would certainly outlive him.

Andy stares at a box TV broadcasting snow and thinks about the Time/Life series of books called *Mysteries of the Unknown*. Actually, he doesn't think about the books, but about the commercials for the books. The ominous, deep-voiced narrator (what dark secrets does he know?), the chiaroscuro lighting (what do those shadows hide?), the ineffable mechanical thunder of the typewriter (what grim portents will it print?), the disconcerting events brought into being (what inscrutable dimensions will invade and conquer our own?).

When his attention is finally drawn away from the TV, does Andy find himself in a motel with not only a dresser, but also an armoire that looks like maybe it's intended for more than just clothing storage? How long do the moteliers expect people to stay in this roadside dive? Does anyone *actually* take all their stuff out of their suitcases, put it in the dresser and the armoire, and then pack everything back up the next day and leave? What's that armoire really used for? Is there like a gate back there leading to probably we'd rather not know where? Is that sound really coming from the television? What kind of place is this?

Well, it isn't a motel.

It's a basement.

The snow-broadcaster really is a box television set sitting on a low, thin, rectangular coffee table. Covering the floor are various large squares of mismatched carpet. The walls are gray cinderblock. The couch Andy sits on is black vinyl, as are the two flanking chairs. There is a wood-burning stove in one corner and a sump pump in the other. Andy wonders how he got here. Wasn't he just in . . . ? But then he looks at the TV again and thinks about the *Mysteries of the Unknown* commercials, thinks about him and his sister, Stefanie, making a mad dash for the power knob because they know once the dread unleashed by those ads grabs hold of you, it doesn't let go willingly. Andy, staring into the interference blizzard, expects a new advertisement to emerge, one that must be stopped, one that will feature him, one that will augur an uncanny age of infinite vertigo that . . .

The alarm clock rings.

Confused, Andy reaches to turn it off, accidentally hits the remote which brings the flatscreen TV to life broadcasting electromagnetic noise (also called "snow"). Andy, with immediacy, recalls an experience he pretty much never experienced, namely the fact that when he was a kid he used to sleepwalk. Normally, Andy was told about his somnambulism either by his mom or dad. One time, though, he discovered he must've been noctambulant because he awakened in his basement, at first wondering where he was, only the light of the box television blizzard giving him any idea, marveling at the fact that his body could take him somewhere without him being in control whatsoever.

Looking away from the TV, Andy sees that he must be in a motel room, though, groggily, he doubts he put any of his stuff in either the dresser or the armoire. He's certain he didn't set the alarm for 4:00 a.m., however. But where he's going and where he's coming from are less certain. Andy has lived so many places, a friend in Lawrence, Kansas, once introduced him this way: "This is Andy, he's from everywhere." Scanning the motel room again, Andy stops on the armoire. He hadn't opened it. He gets the feeling not that he should, but that he will. As if his body had decided. Was the joker who set the clock in there? Was the interior designer who thought, "Why *not* put an overly elaborate piece of furniture in this dump?" It appears Andy will find out. Walking toward this anomaly, why does it sound like the interference is getting louder? Is there something wrong with the speakers? The settings? The wiring? Or, and maybe this isn't true, but it sure seems like there's another television also transmitting snow in here. Putting his hand on the door, when he opens it, will a white light blare through? Will the roar reach an ungodly crescendo, letting any sane person know it's time to do like in *Poltergeist* and shove the tube outside? Or will Andy jump through, his brain wondering why his body's doing this, just as the transmission rights itself?

Will the screen show . . . ?

In the Midwest, a man wakes up in a motel room in 2018 and a boy wakes up in the basement of a house in 1988 at precisely the same time. The man believes he is a boy in a basement, that he's been awakened by television snow, that he ended up where he is because of his sleepwalking, though he doesn't come to that conclusion immediately, meaning he wonders where he is. The boy believes he is a man in a motel room, that he's been awakened by an alarm clock, that he ended up where he is because he's traveling from one nameless place to another, though he doesn't come to that conclusion immediately, meaning he wonders where he is . . . and who set the alarm clock. This boy and this man are the same person. The coincidence is passed off as chance.

Andy wishes Stefanie would've gotten to the power knob quicker. Andy hopes his parents don't tell him about this one.

Standing in front of the mirror, Andy thinks about his friend Simon's paranoia. For whatever reason, Simon thinks that there are cameras hidden behind motel room mirrors and that these cameras were planted by someone named Zimmermann. Simon had, supposedly, run into that name in the way literary and cinematic paranoids stumble upon clues to the big picture, clues which repeat with enough frequency that the character and the audience are subsequently filled with anxiety whenever they hear or see the reference. Consequently, when he can, Simon removes the motel mirror from the wall and looks for two things: (1) a camera, (2) a label that lists the name Zimmermann.

Simon's own name, by the way, is not Simon. He self-applied that name perhaps in an attempt to recreate himself, or perhaps to hide his real identity from *Them*.

Andy, looking into the mirror, does not have this form of paranoia. He does wonder, however, why we (and here he means "humanity") believe people are watching us when what we do is, for the most part, crushingly boring. Currently, for instance, Andy is shaving. If there were a camera recording from behind the glass, and if Zimmermann were tasked with watching the video, he would know by now that Andy almost always starts with the right sideburn area using downward strokes, then with upward strokes does his entire throat area, then back to downward strokes for the left sideburn, leaving him with an oversized Vandyke of soap, which he eliminates with a combination of upward and downward movements, depending, before moving on to his head (which Andy has been stripping clean since he was twenty-three, when his hair began to thin). Unlike his face, Andy does not follow any particular pattern shaving his head, though, over the years, he has learned that a great deal more scraping is necessary to smooth the skullcap. Unfortunately, his skin has never gotten any tougher (alas!), meaning he's just as susceptible to cutting himself as he was the first time. Andy has furthermore learned that the area behind his ears needs special care because, strangely, it can feel shaved when actually it is not, the hair revealing itself later when Andy runs his hands over what he thinks is a completely bald head, only to discover what he hoped not to discover, normally at times when he cannot fix the mistake immediately.

Surely, Zimmermann will be able to use all of this essential knowledge to his enigmatic benefit. He can also use the fact that, after long car trips, Andy often feels oddly greasy and therefore likes to shave and shower, in that order because he has found that if he starts bleeding (a likelihood), either because of a nick, or because he has shaved over a pimple, or whatever, the shower seems to clean out the wound, so he doesn't need to staunch with a tissue and then apply a bandage.

Zimmermann will also be interested in the fact that, after he shaves, Andy will unwrap the tiny soap, ignore the little bottles of shampoo and conditioner (unnecessary for a bald guy), select a washcloth, take a shower, dry himself off with a scratchy towel, make note of the passive aggressive sign that lists how much the towels cost, make note of the sign that asks you to leave your used towel on the floor, drop said towel on the floor, put on his shorts and T-shirt he'll wear to bed, leave the bathroom (shutting off the light in the process), walk into the main room, pull back the blankets, climb inside, and prepare to go to sleep, while, are you serious?, Zimmermann faithfully logs all of this information so he can file reports with the appropriate personnel at the apportioned time which will be used to do what, exactly? Take Andy down? Blackmail Andy? Manipulate Andy in some other way? No, it seems more likely that the Zimmermanns (Zimmermenn?) would have a high rate of ennui-induced suicide if they had to do this for a living, being an absolutely absurd job.

But then, Andy wonders why we always assume the watchers mean us harm. Since the very idea of this paranoia is that we will never meet *Them*, never understand *Their* plan, how come no one ever decides that the conspiracy is neutral? After all, *They* are diligently recording our humdrum, quotidian lives with exactitude, leaving nothing whatsoever out. Doesn't this sound like a cabal of accountants? Or maybe even of archivists? What intrigue could they possibly bring upon us? If anything, we should pity their situation. We should, whenever possible, insert climactic situations into our lives merely to entertain the poor, poor watchers. Ah, Zimmermann! Ah, humanity!

Andy will not, however, think about the fact that the people watching might be . . . benevolent. Knowing that humans often fear loneliness, *They* watch and find ways to inform people that *They*'re out there. Looking in. Caring. Meaning, you're not alone. Meaning, really, you're never alone. If you speak, someone will hear you. If you do something marvelous and wish someone would've seen it, well someone *did* see it. Unfortunately, for reasons that'll never be made plain, *They* are not allowed to fully reveal *Themselves*. But hints to *Their* existence are completely acceptable. For Simon, the name "Zimmermann" and maybe, one day, one day when he least expects it, a camera right behind the mirror to fuel his Romantic paranoia. As for the sleeping Andy, well there is the alarm clock, unassuming, ineffable as the ticking seconds, warmly glowing. Will it burst to life with a message of hope, of togetherness? A positive version of paranoia? Only time will tell . . .

Coincidentally, Zimmermann is a good name for this delusion because *zimmer* in German means "room." The man who watches the room! So you needn't fear a mass suicide from the watchers. Looking on, with that potentially benevolent, though completely unfathomable purpose, one must imagine Zimmermann happy.

Andrew Everett Farkas, on this occasion, does not stop at a motel for the night. Instead, he fights off the expected exhaustion with a large coffee, with loud music, with raucous singing to the loud music, shaking his fist at the motor lodges he passes to show he's defeated them. But when he looks in his rearview mirror, full of hubris, proud that he'll make it all the way to his destination in one go, he wonders what stories he's missing out on by not stopping, wonders if one of those motels would've finally revealed the answer to this perplexing riddle, wonders if one of those motels would've added to the perplexity in an intriguing way. As he continues down the road, all he can do is imagine the rooms he's been in before, the rooms he might check into in the future. What do they look like? If you close your eyes, you can see them. Right there in front of you. Full of unexpected accouterments, full of expected accouterments, and amongst all that stuff, even though, for years, you always had the option for a wakeup call, even though, also for years now, you could use your cell phone's buzzer, amongst everything sits the alarm clock. Sphinxlike.

Inside of the motel room.

Just close your eyes.

You can see it.

Like it's right there in front of you.

for Robert Coover

Everything You Were Looking For

Standing before the drugstore's backroom is a stock boy. Soon, he will open and step through the door. But not yet. For now, he has paused. Paused? Somehow, this moment has become fraught. He's not sure why. As if a great revelation were about to tear through the cosmos and reveal itself to him. The air vibrating. Ridiculous. It was the usual. A shopper, head in the clouds, sure, directed him here. Only this time, it doesn't feel so mundane. Perhaps fate sent him here. Or, anyway, something bigger. And that's why, on this occasion, before he opens the door, before he shuffles into the backroom, the mulleted stock boy puts together not what the customer said, but what the customer, what *all* customers mean when they send him to the backroom to look for something he already knows, and, he assumes, *they* already know, isn't to be had:

"Just back there is a room where everything is. I know it seems unlikely, but it's true. Everything. Right. Back. There. The product I'm currently looking for that's conspicuously absent from the shelf, of course. *Of course*. The merchandise that's on sale, even though it went quickly, even though it was so amazingly priced that the sale itself caused traffic jams, lines around the store, fights, riots, the mayor now drafting legislation forbidding deals like these ever again because they're hazardous to public health, a danger to public safety, and yet, if only you would've retrieved what you definitely have *you know where*, then all of this could've been stopped. Who do you think you're fooling? Come on. And that's not all. The goods that are well stocked out here for everyone to see, that have been well stocked for so long we figure they'll be discontinued soon, guess where else they can be found. The goods that are well stocked, but which sell at a gradual rate, just enough to keep the home office convinced (*Witch Hazel, whodathunkit? don't know what it does, but throw it on the truck, must be the right amount of saps who're, um, drinking this shit? or whatever*), yeah, it's not only available on the shop floor, pal. But there's more. Do you remember that candy bar you ate when you were a kid, seemed like every single day, that soda pop you always drank, neither of which you've seen for years? What, I have to draw you a map? Or do you recall that old remedy, maybe had a bit of a bad reputation (*kid's got himself a case of the gator skin*), but it worked wonders for you, and your life, if you can call it that now, hasn't been right since it . . . were you about to say "vanished"? There's no reason to. You think the list's over? Oh no. The Coca-Cola with cocaine in it, the diet pills with methamphetamine, ephedra, or fenfluramine, the cough syrup made with heroin, every single miracle cure that contained opium, is it for the health and safety of the community that you don't haul 'em out here, put 'em on the shelves, make an endcap, a full-on display, Dr. Pharkas's Phantastic Philter, buy twelve, get a baker's dozen! You're not dealing with dolts. We're in the know. The cigarettes certified by physicians, barely a cough in a carton, oh so mild, sure, they're already faced toward the public, but that's not the only place where they can be found. And what about, oh, you know what I'm talking about, just on the tip of my tongue, it was really, really good, came in a distinctive . . ., heard they don't even make that color anymore, yeah! the commercials, pure genius, though really, if we're being honest here, didn't need to be advertised because, for goodness sakes, I mean, what couldn't it do . . . ? Except it couldn't actually do anything because, of course, it never, right, existed . . . only that's not quite true, now is it? *Is it?!* No, it's not true at all. Because there is one place where you can find it. There is. And you, stock boy, have access to this place. You're the only one, the one and only. Now, I understand, you can't abuse this power. I admire your unwavering, unflinching loyalty to your code. Honorable. If only there were more like you. But on this occasion, pretty please, with sugar on top, get your ass to the backroom and fetch me my shit."

The stock boy stands before the door that, he once thought, led to the backroom. Now, he's not so sure. It feels like a portal to another dimension. It feels like whatever he'll see in there will devastate all he's ever known. He isn't even sure he can open the door. What lies on the other side may be too much for him. Too much. But there is no choice. He must go.

Years later, when the stock boy grows into a stock man, he'll have this exchange with a cashier:

Cashier: "Did you find everything you were looking for?"

Stock Man: "Isn't that an impossibly high bar for a trip to the drugstore?"

For a trip to the drugstore, perhaps. But as for a trip to the backroom, perhaps not. Because, there in the future, when he throws open the door and plunges into the darkness beyond, after he's finally able to force his eyes open, with thanks to the many, many gurus who've instructed him in the mystic ways, he'll find everything he was looking for, everything you were looking for, everything everyone was looking for. He just hadn't known how to look until now.

An Essay About Nothing

Once

The first time I taught *Waiting for Godot* (1953), without explanation, I showed *Seinfeld*'s "The Chinese Restaurant" (1991) to the class.

About the latter, an episode where Jerry, George, and Elaine wait to get a table so they can eat before they see a screening of *Plan 9 from Outer Space* (1959), where they never get seated, finally leaving fed up, but unfed, I asked the students what *Seinfeld* was about. They were ready. They knew.

"It's about nothing," said my students. Then they quoted the line:

"It's a show about nothing."

Steven Robert Byrd (Steve to his friends) arrives for Advanced Fiction Writing (6:00–8:30 p.m.) and takes his seat in the classroom.

"I'd very much like to sit down, but I don't quite know how to go about it," says Pozzo.

"Could I be of any help?" says Estragon.

"If you asked me perhaps," says Pozzo.

"What?" says Estragon.

"If you asked me to sit down," says Pozzo.

"Can't look at the menu now, I gotta be at the table," says Jerry.

"Everything's gotta be just so all the time with you, doesn't it?" says Elaine.

It's not *his* seat, but Steve probably thinks of it as his.

About *Waiting for Godot,* the students asked why Vladimir and Estragon do the same thing every day when they don't have to.

I pointed out to the students that they sat in the same places every day, even though I'd never given them desk assignments, even though there were more desks than pupils.

⤙

As undergrads, Steve and I had a number of classes together. This was by design.

"I sometimes wonder if we wouldn't have been better off alone, each one for himself. We weren't made for the same road," says Estragon.

"I can't go to a bad movie by myself. What am I gonna make sarcastic comments to strangers?" says Jerry.

Also as undergrads, Steve and I had the same shirt. This was *not* by design.

"You must be happy too, deep down, if only you knew it," says Vladimir.
"Happy about what?" says Estragon.
"To be back with me again," says Vladimir.

Steve did not like it that he and I had the same shirt; I liked it very much.

"I just can't believe the way people are. What is it with humanity? What kind of a world do we live in?" says George.

Once I realized Steve and I had the same shirt, and once I realized Steve did not like that we had the same shirt, I wore it every time we had class together.

"Happy about what?" says Estragon.
"To be back with me again," says Vladimir.
"Would you say so?" says Estragon.

Or as often as hygienically possible. Which, as an undergrad guy, was pretty often.

"Look at his little outfit. It's all so coordinated. The little socks match the little shirt. I really hate this guy," says George.

"It'd be better if we parted," says Estragon.

The students had no problems with *Seinfeld*.

The students had the usual problems with *Waiting for Godot*.

For example, Vladimir and Estragon are so similar they can't be told apart, everyone said. Showing pictures of various productions didn't help:

"They even dress the same!"

Steve how I see him: six-foot-two, long brown hair, red van dyke beard, stalwart of build, wearing black combat boots, blue jeans, and either a flannel or a gray Notre Dame T-shirt (though he doesn't care about sports).

But since Steve and I have the same shirt . . .

"He has stinking breath and I have stinking feet," says Estragon.

"Cartwright, Cartwright," says the maître d'.

Then Steve *could* be wearing a midnight blue, long-sleeve Henley (sometimes called a waffle shirt), instead.

And Steve *could* now be looking at this shirt as if, of its own volition, it'd wrapped itself around him.

"Five, ten minutes," says the maître d'.

"Your only hope left is to disappear," says Vladimir.

"Goddamnit," Steve will say when I join him. Or, will likely say when I join him. Or, might plan to say when I join him, if only now he's remembered that we have the same shirt.

"Nothing to be done," says Estragon.

"I'm beginning to come round to that opinion," says Vladimir.

"Where am I? Is this a dream? What in God's name is going on here?" says Elaine.

And I hope to say: "Hey Steve! Same shirt!"

❦

The students complained that the play takes place in the middle of nowhere, a landscape devoid of character.

Pointing out that Samuel Beckett fought against producers who wanted to give *Godot* a more specific setting certainly didn't help.

❦

"What's it like?" says Pozzo.

"It's indescribable. It's like nothing. There's nothing," says Vladimir.

The classroom where Steve sits:

Rectangular with a large, gray conference table in the center surrounded by hard plastic chairs that are maroon with exposed steel supports. A chalkboard takes up the entirety of one long wall. The other long wall is blank.

"I hate this place. I don't know why we came here. I'm never coming back here again," says Elaine.

The reason I can't tell you what shirt Steve's wearing is because I have yet to join him in the classroom.

"So there you are again," says Vladimir.

"Am I?" says Estragon.

"This isn't plans one through eight from outer space, this is *Plan 9*. This is the one that worked. The worst movie ever made," says Jerry.

In the Classic Films course Steve and I took, a student asked what he needed to do to get an A on a paper, since he (the student) had tried and tried with no luck. The professor said he didn't think it was all that difficult, seeing as how there were two freshmen in the class who'd gotten A's on all the papers.

Rather loudly, and quite obliviously, I said: "Hey Steve! Is that us?"

After a pause, Steve said: "Yes, Andy. That's us."

"It'd be better if we parted," says Estragon.

"I just can't believe the way people are. What is it with humanity?" says George.

Thinking of the Classic Films class, Steve might not have walked into Advanced Fiction Writing. Instead, it could be American Literature 1945–Present, or Literary Theory, or the aforementioned movie course.

"Forget all I said. I don't remember exactly what it was, but you may be sure there wasn't a word of truth in it," says Pozzo.

So then the classroom is squarish with orderly rows and columns of desks consisting of variably colored, hard plastic chairs and brown writing surfaces connected by thin metal pipes. There is a chalkboard and a table at the front for the instructor. The other walls are blank.

"Mr. Cohen is always here," says the maître d'.

"He's always here? What does that mean? What does that mean?" says Elaine.

And, of course, the biggest problem the students had: the fact that nothing happens.

"You haven't even grasped the worst of it," I pointed out. "According to literary critic Vivian Mercier, in *Waiting for Godot*, 'Nothing happens, twice.'"

While sitting in the classroom, perhaps Steve thinks about the time I said:

"Do you remember when Beowulf tore Grendel's arm off and beat him with it?"

"That didn't happen, Andy."

"In an instant all will vanish and we'll be alone once more, in the midst of nothingness," says Vladimir.

"The worst movie ever made," says Jerry.

"It didn't?"

"No, Andy. Beowulf ripped his arm off, and that's all."

"We know them, I tell you. You forget everything," says Vladimir.

"Remember when you first went out to eat with your parents? Remember?" says Elaine.

"Oh . . . But wasn't that awesome, though?"

"That thing that didn't happen? Yeah, Andy, I guess that was awesome."

⁂

"And oh, by the way, what you're saying, then, is that it's a play about nothing."

The students were not impressed by my ruse.

⁂

"Yes, now I remember, yesterday evening we spent blathering about nothing in particular," says Estragon.

"Five, ten minutes," says the maître d'.

While sitting in the classroom, perhaps Steve thinks about the many times when I said:

"Hey Steve, do you mind if I tell you what happens in this book I'm reading?"

"Yeah, I do. I plan on reading that book."

"In the meantime let us try and converse calmly, since we are incapable of keeping silent," says Estragon.

"Oh . . . Well, uh, what happens is . . ."

"You know, we're living in a society! We're supposed to act in a civilized way!" says George.

"So, that aside, you're going to tell me anyway?"
"That's right. And by the way: Hey Steve!"
"What?"
"Same shirt!"
Beat.
"Goddamnit."

Twice

The meeting after I informed my students that they sat in the same seats each day without ever being told to, I pointed out that they'd done it again.

"Don't let's do anything. It's safer," says Estragon.

Steve in the classroom perhaps doesn't think about what I'm wearing because he's not wearing the midnight blue, long-sleeve Henley.

"You ever notice how happy people are when they finally get a table? They feel so special because they've been chosen. It's enough to make you sick," says Elaine.

Or, perhaps Steve delusionally believes today will be different, that I won't be wearing the midnight blue, long-sleeve Henley, that I won't get to use my favorite line.

"People are bloody ignorant apes," says Estragon.

Except it doesn't matter what Steve has on. At a certain point, he realized when I wore that shirt, the midnight blue, long-sleeve Henley, I wore it to get under his skin.

"There's fifty dollars in it for you if you do," says Jerry.

Sometimes, when I say, "Hey Steve! Same shirt!" it's probably confusing for other people because our shirts are not at all the same.

I told my students that they sat in the same places because our sense of order is rooted in knowing what comes next. When we know what comes next, the world is easily understandable. But when things change, the world becomes alien. To fight off that absurdity, people will even endure odious routines.

Of course, Steve could always get rid of his midnight blue, long-sleeve Henley.

"Let's go," says Estragon.
"We can't," says Vladimir.
"Why not?" says Estragon.
"We're waiting for Godot," says Vladimir.

"Can't look at the menu now, I gotta be at the table," says Jerry.
"Everything's gotta be just so all the time with you, doesn't it?" says Elaine.

All he'd have to do is throw the shirt away. Or give it to someone else.

"What a sorry exhibition that was," says Jerry.

"I can't go on like this," says Estragon.
"That's what you think," says Vladimir.

But, of course, Steve will not get rid of the midnight blue, long-sleeve Henley. "Goddamnit," says Steve.

When we are sent reeling, when the world becomes an alien place, we even lose our sense of self, making us wonder not just if we know who we are, but if we ever knew. Since we've been wrong before, we could be wrong again. And since people have so much in common, what actually differentiates us?

"Excuse me, I'm expecting a call. Costanza," says George.

"Yes, I just got a call. I yell, 'Cartwright, Cartwright,' just like that. Nobody came up; I hang up," says the maître d'.

Actually, I am wrong. It's not Steve sitting in the classroom waiting for me. It's me in the classroom waiting for Steve.

"Forget all I said. I don't remember exactly what it was, but you may be sure there wasn't a word of truth in it," says Pozzo.

Steve is normally late; I am normally early.

"He has stinking breath and I have stinking feet," says Estragon.
"Nobody ever recognizes us," says Vladimir.

So, unless it's an off day, I am the one sitting in the classroom.

"He yelled 'Cartwright,' " says George.
"Who's *Cartwright*?" says Jerry.
"I'm *Cartwright*," says George.
"You're not *Cartwright*," says Jerry.
"Of course I'm not *Cartwright!*" says George. Costanza.

Once we have lost the world (*Godot's* nowhere setting) and ourselves (Vladimir and Estragon being so similar), we desperately reach back for the time when everything made sense. To no avail.

꙰

"Remember when you first went out to eat with your parents? Remember?" says Elaine.

"So, that aside, you're going to tell me anyway?"
"That's right."

"We were respectable in those days," says Vladimir.

Steve *could* be wearing a midnight blue, long-sleeve Henley (sometimes called a waffle shirt).

"It was such a treat to go and they serve you this different food that you never saw before," says Elaine.

"Do you remember when Beowulf tore Grendel's arm off and beat him with it?"
"That didn't happen, Andy."

"Tomorrow, when I wake, or think I do, what shall I say of today? That with Estragon my friend, at this place, until the fall of night, I waited for Godot?" says Vladimir.

"Hey Steve! Same shirt!"
"Goddamnit."

"And they put it in front of you and it was such a delicious and exciting adventure," says Elaine.

"That thing that didn't happen? Yeah, Andy, I guess that was awesome."

"Habit is a great deadener," says Vladimir.

Steve did not like it that he and I had the same shirt; I liked it very much.

"And now I just feel like a big, sweaty hog waiting for them to fill up the trough," says Elaine.

"Hey Steve! Is that us?"

"Hey Steve!"

Long after they could be expected to remember, I told the students they'd done it again. They'd all sat in the same seats.

I told them that although it approaches the topic, *Waiting for Godot* isn't about nothing. It's about the fact that people are constantly waiting for someone to deliver them from their situations, when they should actually do something themselves.

I told them that *Seinfeld* isn't about nothing either. It's a show about the lives of four New Yorkers and their friends and acquaintances.

And now I tell you this essay isn't about nothing. Because everything is about something and never about nothing, no matter how hard we try. We can only ever orbit nothing, we can never arrive.

After seeing the unfortunate movie, *Eragon* (2006), and hearing that it was supposed to be the beginning of a trilogy, Steve said to me:
"I think that's the first of one movie."

"Five, ten minutes," says the maître d'.

"The tears of the world are a constant quantity. For each one who begins to weep somewhere else another stops. The same is true of the laugh. Let us not then speak ill of our generation, it is not any unhappier than its predecessors. Let us not speak well of it either. Let us not speak of it at all," says Pozzo.

It is not me sitting in that classroom anymore.

I'm not wearing the midnight blue, long-sleeve Henley (which I haven't owned in some time).

And I'm not waiting for Steve.

"Five, ten minutes," says the maître d'.

"I tell you I wasn't doing anything," says Estragon.

"Perhaps you weren't. But it's the way of doing it that counts, the way of doing it, if you want to go on living," says Vladimir.

Where am I now? Nowhere.

Who am I now? I can hardly tell.

"Five, ten minutes," says the maître d'.

"Nothing happens, nobody comes, nobody goes, it's awful!" says Estragon.

But once in a while, I can see myself there, wearing the midnight blue, long-sleeve Henley, my arms crossed, a smirk on my face, waiting to bug Steve in any number of ways. If Steve was your friend, you'd do the same.

And in that moment, I pretend I know exactly where and who I am.

"Five, ten minutes," says the maître d'.

But then the moment's gone and I'm adrift again.

"That passed the time," says Vladimir.

"It would have passed in any case," says Estragon.

"Yes, but not so rapidly," says Vladimir.

When Hamburger Station Is Busy

Thought Problem

Whenever I go to Hamburger Station for lunch with my dad and I point out there's nobody there, he says, "It's busier at dinnertime."

Whenever I go to Hamburger Station for dinner with my dad and I point out there's nobody there, he says, "It's busier at lunchtime."

So, when is Hamburger Station busy?

Solution #1: *Hamburger Station is never busy.*

When I think about Hamburger Station, what comes to mind is the eight-foot fiberglass horse (named American Red), the covered wagon, the font on the sign that could be called Clapboard Bold, the interior that looks like a combination of a Wild West saloon and a 1950s diner: some of the linoleum counter's stools are actually saddles, there are burlap sacks of potatoes, burlap sacks of onions, a rough wooden floor, inconceivably no one's ever been thrown through the front window at the end of a brawl (a fact that's always bothered me), a stainless steel flattop grill covered in mouth-watering grease, deep fryers for the fresh-cut fries, a wall menu with those plastic letters and numbers, employees in white T-shirts, an old cash register, booths, the malt vinegar for the fresh-cut fries, and the burgers. The burgers. These aren't those lousy meatloaf-tasting sliders from White Castle or Krystal. No way. White Castle and Krystal are the elementary school cafeteria version. Hamburger Station burgers. They're two and a half inch squares. Piled high with onions, pickles, mustard. Dinner roll for a bun. Get yourself a Speed Pack (two burgers, fries, lemonade). Yeah. That right there. That right there . . .

That's what I think about.

But, uh, right. Not much in the way of other patrons, I mention to my dad.

He takes a sip of lemonade.

He responds in an unconcerned deadpan.

Solution #2: *Hamburger Station is only busy when I'm not there.*

Although the Menches Brothers, Frank and Charles, invented the hamburger (which is what Northeast Ohioans *actually* believe, even if the Akron Hamburger Hearings of 2006 graciously awarded that honor to Charles Nagreen of Seymour, Wisconsin), others perfected what no one calls a plain old sandwich anymore. In other words, the Menches were like the Titans in Greek mythology. Interesting, sure. But what we really want are the Olympians. The line of succession, then, goes like this: the fabled Peppy Service Lunch begat Marvin "Pop" Thacker, who went on to create the exalted Thacker's Hamburgs; Thacker's Hamburgs begat Jim Lowe, who went on to found the renowned Hamburger Station.

With such an illustrious history, you can imagine that Jim Lowe, in his incongruous cowboy hat of immeasurable gallons, his inexplicable shitkicker boots (having spent most of his life in burger joints in the Buckeye State, not pastures in Texas), his large glasses that helped him see more than the normal human, well, you can imagine that Jim Lowe had the power of prophesy. And it could be that when, as a little kid, I met him, a meeting I do not remember, a meeting only related to me by my dad, a man who once said, "When I told you honesty was the best policy, I was lying," during this supposed meeting, the legendary founder of Hamburger Station perhaps had this to say to me:

"Son, don't be skeered, but I can see the future. Yessiree Bob. And what I see off there in the heretofore, and this is the Simon pure, is twenty Hamburger Stations, son, twenty Hamburger Stations spanning Northeast Ohio. A purty thought. Yet somehow, and now, I don't rightly know why, somehow, and I don't mind jawin' at you like this on account of no-way will you recollect what I'm clapping down, somehow, anytime you come in, ya little varmint, a fandango it will not be. Fact a business, it'll be a ghost town. Me, I won't be afeared. When all you can hear are the winds a-howlin', the sand a-blowin', the tumbleweeds a-rollin', whereas my friendly fellers will be full of flusteration, I won't be because I'll know what's a-comin'—you. It'll be you. Maybe you and yer paw. Maybe you and one of them scalawags in yer posse. But that's all. Hain't no one else will be here. And for the rest of yer dadgummed life, you'll wonder how this could be. Hamburger Stations far as the eye can see; nobody

inside. Whipper-snapper, that there's yer fate. Why's for the folks up the dox-
ology works to know."

I tell Scott Schulman, a friend of mine, about me and my dad's routine.

He says that can't be. It can't just be the fate of Farkas. Because he and his
dad, they have the same routine.

Solution #3: *Hamburger Station is busy at an undisclosed,
perhaps undisclosable time.*

The grease on the flattop grill sizzles and I am enthralled not only by the sa-
vory smell, but by the mystery . . .

In this hipster-dominated era, when people try to one-up each other by being the first to adopt that which will become a trend, either by finding something brand new or by reviving something old (thus the reason for Pabst Blue
Ribbon's re-ascendancy once upon a time), you might think my dad and I
fit right in, that we're trailblazers, that we're tastemakers. The grease, oh that
smell making my mouth water, does not agree. To explain, some Hamburger
Station lore:

For years, Hamburger Station didn't carry ketchup. The burgers were
served "neat," which meant pickles and (lots of) onions, with squeeze bottles
of mustard throughout the restaurant and malt vinegar for the fresh-cut fries.
But no ketchup. Jim Lowe liked to tell a story about a customer who would
come in always asking for that red garbage. Finally, Lowe put it on a burger,
and supposedly the man said he'd never ask for ketchup again. According to
Lowe, ketchup and the grease Hamburger Station uses on the burgers do not
mix well because the tomato product screws up the pH balance making the
whole thing taste bad. Being so important, it's probably no surprise then that
the grease recipe is a closely guarded secret.

In fact, during his lifetime, Lowe was the only one who knew how to
make it.

(But who knows how to make it now . . .?)

And so, the reason my dad and I can't claim membership in an exclusive
club is because a place like Hamburger Station, that bases the taste of its primary product on a secret-recipe grease, that refuses to change how the burgers
are dressed even once they started carrying ketchup and mayonnaise (treating
the bottles like they're full of some infectious disease), meaning Hamburger
Station has willfully accepted losing customers in order to adhere to their ideal

of what a burger *ought to be*, well a place like that isn't interested in being busy, and asking when Hamburger Station is immediately proves I *just don't get it*. Likely, then, the people who do *get it* are initiated into the secret society, the *real* Hamburger Station, where the mysteries are revealed (obviously one of which is the recipe for the grease), the adepts later entering their perhaps underground chapter room, full to capacity (a capacity that won't be giving McDonald's a run for its money, but who would want to, you?! then what in the world are you doing here?!), where they gawk at flatscreens depicting these lunkheads (Farkas? What kind of name is that anyway?!) who think they know what it means to be dedicated to Hamburger Station.

But if this is the case, if Hamburger Station is merely a front for the Ancient Western Order of the Buckeroos of the Mystic Grease, then my family is a splinter faction that hides in plain sight. After all, my mom, dad, sister, and yours truly all hate ketchup, and since, when we're there, no one else ever appears to be, that means the restaurant itself serves as our own private (one might even say *secret*) chapter room, and perhaps, when we have quorum, *that's* when Hamburger Station is busy.

Solution #4: *Hamburger Station is only "busy" relative to other times.*

My dad holds up an onion ring and comments on the fact that it's bigger than one of the hamburgers. This comparison seems important to him, so important he often brings it up. But me, I'm thinking of another comparison, a comparison that focuses on the word "busier."

It could be that my question, "When is Hamburger Station busy?" is the wrong one. After all, when my dad says, "It's busier at [lunchtime/dinnertime]," he might just be speaking comparatively. For instance, if I go to Hamburger Station with my dad for lunch one day, and then go there with my friends John Schloman and Scott Schulman for dinner the next day, then technically my dad is right: it's busier (though not necessarily "busy").

But a different problem rears its head here. As teenagers, John, Scott, and I often ate with our families, met up later on, and then ate again. Contrarily, we sometimes knew that we'd be eating with our families later and that there wouldn't be time afterwards, so we went before we were to rendezvous with our families. In each instance, what meal were John, Scott, and I having? If it was neither lunch, nor dinner, then could we justifiably call when we were eating lunchtime or dinnertime?

This confusion reminds me of a story. One day, at school, John was asked how his brother was doing. Since John's brother, Bill, is considerably older than John, and since the person who had inquired about his brother was younger than John, John wondered how this person knew his brother. Anyway, John said that Bill was fine. "No, not Bill. The other one." Having no other brother, John was confused. "What's his name? With the sideburns. Scott! How's Scott?" It was then that he realized what'd happened. John's last name being Schloman, Scott's last name being Schulman, both names being a collision of "shhh" and "el" and "man" sounds, they must be the same: Schuloman. Yeah, that's right. Or, anyway, close enough.

But close enough isn't good enough here. So much as John and Scott aren't brothers, the meals we were eating were neither lunch, nor dinner, meaning for us the times weren't lunchtime or dinnertime.

Of course, the fact that teenage boys eat a lot isn't news. So, maybe it doesn't matter what meal we happened to be having. Instead, what matters is the time. And whereas those times, lunch and dinner, may be variable (in my adult years, I've lived and continue to live on a much different schedule than others), we have a general idea of when they are.

I don't think my dad's thought problem is semantic, however. If it were, he probably wouldn't care *when* Hamburger Station was busy, or if it were ever busy at all. Seeing as how Jim Lowe's legacy is one of my dad's favorite restaurants, though, he does care. Since he cares, his fun can't be nihilistic, ultimately auguring Hamburger Station's doom. Yeah, I've let myself get bogged down in meals and times, when something else is at work . . .

Again, my dad holds up an onion ring and I finally understand that his constant observation is connected to his thought problem. The reason my dad always references the other time, the time when we're not there, is to create a kind of circular logic, as round as the onion ring, the onion ring that isn't just physically bigger than the burgers (which are square), but also figuratively, since within that ring, though we will never truly learn when Hamburger Station is busy, Jim Lowe's restaurant will go on forever.

Solution #5: *Hamburger Station is simultaneously always busy and never busy.*

Whereas I do not recall meeting Jim Lowe, I do remember, when I was a little kid, meeting and befriending a different employee, someone I always looked forward to talking to whenever we went to Hamburger Station, a really, really great guy, you could just tell by his name. His name was Andy. Later, of course, Andy would go on to collect college degrees at Kent State University, the University of Tennessee, the University of Alabama, and the University of Illinois at Chicago and become a creative writing professor at Washburn University. Later, of course, Andy would go on to move up in the ranks at Hamburger Station, from order taker to cook to trainer to assistant manager to manager to general manager, before retiring. Whenever they met, the two Andys got along wonderfully, each time happy to engage in their favorite activity: comparing burger bellies. Who could eat more Hamburger Station burgers? They didn't know, but they were going to find out.

This unadulterated love for Hamburger Station leads me to the fact that just about everyone I know loves the place. And, often, just about everyone *they* know loves the place. Even the famous rock band The Black Keys, who hail from Akron, when loading the cover of their third studio album, *Rubber Factory* (2004), with as many hometown landmarks as they could, included Hamburger Station. Not Swenson's or Skyway or Bob's Hamburg or Mr. Hero (home of the Romanburger, which comes on a sub roll, has two patties next to each other, both atop slices of salami) or any of the root beer stands or any of the historic joints like Manner's Big Boy, Lujan's, Pogo, The Varsity, Dilly's, The Flame, or Kamper's, no, The Black Keys chose Hamburger Station (well, they also chose The Corral, home of the NiteMare, a burger that includes a thick slice of chipped chopped ham, but still).

And yet, every time my dad and I go, we have no problem running through our routine. Hamburger Station appears to have taken Yogi Berra's absurdity and turned it into reality: "Nobody goes there anymore. It's too crowded."

From the world of physics, then, I offer two possibilities. First, Erwin Schrödinger famously used a box, a cat, and a poison trap that has a fifty percent chance of triggering in order to explain the problem of measuring a photon. With the box closed, you're not sure if the cat is alive or dead and therefore it is simultaneously alive *and* dead, though that is impossible. What is the point of this thought experiment? The point is that the same is the case for photons: without measuring them (the metaphorical opening of the box), they act like both particles and waves, even though that is as impossible as a cat being both alive and dead. But when you measure photons as if they were particles, they act like particles; when you measure photons as if they were waves, they act like waves. I argue, then, that Hamburger Station, with its many confessed fans, is constantly simultaneously busy and not busy. My own experience, being a drop in the bucket, is irrelevant.

Much as I find that previous argument unsatisfying, Hugh Everett III found the Copenhagen interpretation of physics unsatisfying, since it's impossible for light to be both a particle and a wave simultaneously. And so, my second argument comes from Dr. Everett: the many-worlds interpretation (MWI) of physics. In the MWI, every time a particular action could have multiple outcomes, all of those outcomes take place in separate universes. For instance, anytime my dad and I go to Hamburger Station, it could either be busy or not busy, and therefore it is both, though in separate, unbridgeable realities. When my dad says that Hamburger Station is busier at lunchtime, or that it's busier at dinnertime, since I cannot access those times in the moment, what he is actually telling me is that in some other reality, Hamburger Station is, indeed, busy, but neither of us can experience that universe. Maybe that's for the better. Here, we get our Speed Packs quicker.

Back in a less theoretical version of Jim Lowe's legacy, after eating many, many hamburgers, Andy and Andy, to determine who indeed has the bigger burger belly, turn to an outside judge: my dad. My dad, accepting this solemn duty, rules that both Andys have won. The prize, of course, is a hamburger.

Solution #6: *Hamburger Station is always busy.*

At the writing of this essay, I admit, I'm afraid Hamburger Station isn't long for this world. Whereas I knew of six locations, there may have been as many as ten at one point (Jim Lowe never reaching the twenty he predicted). But now there are two. The ones my dad and I went to the most, near Midway Plaza on Britain Road in East Akron and on State Road in Cuyahoga Falls, are both gone. Whenever I'm back in town, we head to Ellet, a neighborhood in Southeast Akron, for our Hamburger Station fix. It doesn't have a counter to sit at, just booths, like any other fast food joint (the building possibly being a defunct Wendy's franchise). It does have one saddle stool probably to remind people like me about the excitement we felt sitting on them as kids. But none of the other accouterments are to be found.

Of course, after getting our Speed Packs, my dad and I go through our routine.

Honestly, I wish, on occasion at least, we weren't able to. Then I wouldn't have to fear the end of Hamburger Station.

But perhaps I don't have to worry after all. Perhaps the problem isn't that there are fewer Hamburger Stations now, or that there are fewer customers. Instead, the problem is that I'm approaching time the wrong way. According to Massachusetts Institute of Technology physicist Max Tegmark, time is an illusion brought on by perception, not something fundamental to the universe:

"We can portray our reality as either a three-dimensional place where stuff happens over time, or as a four-dimensional place where nothing happens—and if it really is the second picture, then change really is an illusion, because there's nothing that's changing; it's all just there—past, present, future.

"So life is like a movie, and space-time is like the DVD [...] There's nothing about the DVD itself that is changing in any way, even though there's all this drama unfolding in the movie."

If Professor Tegmark is right, then we have found the solution to the thought problem. To celebrate I propose a shindig that will require almost nothing of the partiers, because, having been there before, my attendance is already guaranteed—and my dad will be there, and my mom will be there, and my sister, Stefanie, will be there, and the not-brothers John Schloman and Scott Schulman will be there, and Jim Lowe will definitely be there, as will the other Andy, and even if you've never been, as long as you plan to go sometime in the future, then you will be there, too. And when we meet, finally, we will meet at the time when Hamburger Station is busy.

Last Year at Chapel Hill Mall

"I have another game to suggest instead..."

What game? If this were a movie. So, if this *were* a movie, it'd only be available on VHS, poor copy, bad tracking, picture flipping, but through the visual static you'd see the protagonist (forties, bald, Shuron Ronsir glasses, fireplug build, Hawaiian-shirted) sitting on the patio of a bar obviously not worth showing, focus shallow, the soundtrack coming up, something from the '80s, Hall & Oates, as it turns out, "Maneater," though it's unclear if the lead can hear the song, or if only the audience can, as Baldy drinks a beer, briefly talks (inaudible) to characters not in the frame, the music perhaps too loud and... something seems off about it, really off (how come there are no vocals?), as the shot changes, Baldy's point of view, at first hazy, our "hero" not quite focusing on what's in front of him, but as the picture sharpens (as best it can considering the degraded technology), the distorted soundtrack throbs, hisses, echoes, slows way down (still no singing), and there, across the street, the haze lifted, *just right there* across the street, what's that? oh, Chapel Hill Mall (the water tower says so), yes, Chapel Hill Mall lies dying.

"I know a game I always win."

But how can I lose, as I watch the black-and-white film on a continual loop, since, to my memory, I never was a mall rat, so I couldn't possibly care about Chapel Hill's demise. If this work dealt with my usual hangouts, it'd take place in diners, or coffee shops, or bars, or bookstores, or movie theatres, or bowling alleys, or video rental stores, or comic/games stores. Not a mall, never a mall, as I watch Alain Robbe-Grillet and Alain Resnais' *Last Year at Marienbad* (1961), black-and-white, continual loop, unexpected invasion of emotions about Chapel Hill putting me in the position of A (the female main character), who says she didn't meet X (the male main character) last year, didn't make plans with him to leave M (possibly her husband), didn't even go to the place where their paths supposedly crossed, and therefore hasn't forgotten X because she has no more feelings for him than she'd have for a random person you might meet at, say, a mall (is that a giant wall of snow, or more bad tracking?) — malls which I have been to before, of course, Chapel Hill the most, hands down, but I don't particularly give a damn about any of them.

"If you can't lose, it's not a game!"

"I can lose . . ."

Baldy now stands outside an entrance to the mall . . . and opens the door.

". . . but I always win."

Once again . . . you walk on, once again, through this thundering power plant, down these yellow cinderblock corridors, this secret passage (though unhidden), out onto and then along this grand thoroughfare, past these kiosks, these snack food stands, these stores (stores succeeding stores succeeding stores) providing most of the ornamentation, otherwise white and gray tile, glass, molded plastic benches, simple white and gray ceiling, a black wishing well fountain, in this structure of another decade, no, indeed, of another century, this prodigious, stately, stream-lined, amiable, or maybe just friendly, perhaps the friendliest *mall, yes, yes, as the advertisements once said, "The friendliest mall of all, Chapel Hill Mall," once again . . .*

Maybe the movie was recorded over another because now there's a team of teenage baseball players wearing ear protection instead of caps with their backs to the camera, turning, throwing baseballs, to whom we can't see as the balls seem like they'll come through the screen . . .

"The first time I saw you was in the gardens of . . ."

Remarkably, A and X are not in Marienbad, nor were they necessarily in Marienbad last year, and as Baldy walks through Chapel Hill Mall, the familiar, simple, horizontal plan becomes fluid, wings emerge next to our protagonist, bend in on themselves, then vanish; stores appear, disappear, reappear (though slightly different), as if each step increases the complexity of the blueprint, as if the modulating, corrupted saxophone controls the physical space, as if memories were experienced not in your mind, but corporeally in the

world, with all of their inaccuracies, revisions, duplications, elisions, confab-
ulations, even their bad tracking.

". . . was in the gardens of Frederiksbad."

But perhaps it doesn't matter where they met. Having lived so many places,
I've been to malls all over the US, and each time I walk into one, there's a moment when I believe I'm in Chapel Hill, when the instantly recognizable floor
plan unfolds in front of me, when I think I could close my eyes and name each
store in succession as I passed, meaning, ultimately, I feel like I'm home, feel
like I could just run outside, get in my car, and in about fifteen minutes be back
at the house I grew up in . . .

"I tell you it's impossible. I've never been to Frederiksbad."

This warm sensation does not last. Soon, the actual mall asserts its presence, Baldy walking through an anonymous space, past stores without names,
labeled with bland descriptors (Store, Other Store, Antepenultimate Store,
Penultimate Store, Ultimate Store, Gotcha: A Joke Store), meaning I feel as if
I'm nowhere, nowhere in particular, a vast emptiness, a vacuum, and whereas
the shops Baldy passes appear full of merchandise, something tells us, as the
soundtrack stops and restarts still without lyrics, if he went inside the "employees" would look at each other, would blink, would wonder, justifiably,
what he's doing there.

"Well, then it was somewhere else, maybe . . ."

And yet, this might make it sound as if my hometown mall is the outlier,
the one I remember, the one I want to go to. But it is not. When I'm in other
malls, yes, there is a moment when I believe I'm in Chapel Hill. However,
when I'm in Chapel Hill, I'm soon reminded of every other mall, meaning,
even when I'm fifteen minutes from home, it seems like I could be absolutely
anywhere else, I could be far, far from the house I grew up in. How can this be?
My answer: because Chapel Hill is every mall and every mall is Chapel Hill.
Having felt this same confusion at Rolling Acres and Randall Park, and having
watched as those malls died, I've already felt the pain, felt the sadness, felt the
loss of Chapel Hill, though really I felt nothing, nothing at all.

". . . maybe at Karlstadt, at Marienbad, or at Baden-Salsa—or even here,
in . . ."

As the camera pulls back, the headset-wearing teenage baseball team continues to play catch, though now we see they're in a power plant surrounded by

gigantic diesel engines, as the balls are thrown, apparently, from those off-screen . . .

"In the summer of 1929, we had freezing weather for a week."

The arctic soundtrack could be an instrumental version of "Maneater," though that doesn't entirely explain the distorted warbling, the echoes, the characters in the black-and-white world seemingly on permanent holiday (using the British definition of the word), wandering through the resort gardens, but how are they lit?, the people casting long shadows, the trees no shadows at all, while in the color film Baldy traverses the mall solo, sparkling reflections from a glitter ball, toward a snowman, so maybe a winter wonderland instead of disco, the shops morphing around Baldy (a movie theatre becomes a department store becomes a vacant front), a twenty-foot-tall snowman, top hat, scarf, broom held like a halberd, eyes aglow and blinking when he speaks, the guardian of Christmas . . .

"It's a matter of chance: we always come back here."

Which is true. Growing up, Christmas centered on Chapel Hill Mall; we always came back, no matter how long we'd been gone, often returning with Aunt CC to do the shopping, and now, when I think about it, the holiday season stretches infinitely there, as if I could walk in at any time and see Santa Claus, but more importantly, much more importantly, I could see Archie the Snowman. No other mall had Archie, the gentle giant of Christmas, whom we asked for gifts after making our way past cottony snow, past ice ponds made of mirrors, past animatronic elves skating, tinkering, cavorting, past candy castles, up onto the platform that held the microphone through which you spoke to Archie towering above you, his arms now extended, trying to spread cheer and joy, trying to hug the world. At the end, there were gumdrops.

"But I've already been here before."

"Is it a place you like?"

"Me . . . ?"

Though Archie's holiday might be the wrong one, since, if I am actually interested in Chapel Hill, my interest isn't nostalgic, but ironic, even morbid, as I mix my replay of Last Year at Marienbad with YouTube tours of ghost malls from across the country, wishing I could be there, wishing I could haunt those ruins, while the camera seems to attack A who screams, "You're raving!" and X shouts, "No! No! No!" remembering that one interpretation of

Robbe-Grillet/Resnais' film is that the characters are phantoms forced to repeat the same actions forever, a love affair with no history or future, more
suited to Halloween than Christmas, thunder exploding, sinister lightning
forking behind a twenty-foot-tall scarecrow Archie, his arms extended not
to hug the world, but to horrify, dominate, his eyes glowing red, his voice a
cacophonous roar, Baldy cowering in his Hawaiian shirt, arms blocking his
face, the winter wonderland now a wasteland, as the eerie, lyrics-less music
drones on, unceasing. Only, maybe it's the bad tracking, the visual static, but
the whole thing comes off as cheesy, more rubber-suit Godzilla than anything
that'd give you nightmares, and I think of the Archie my dad found in a storage
space years later, after the yuletide giant had been missing for a while, a broken down old Christmas decoration badly in need of rewiring. So he rewired
the snowman. And once again kids looked up to Archie during the holidays.
Though not me. I wasn't a kid anymore.
    "But I've already been here before."
    "Is it a place you like?"
    "Me? No, not particularly. It's a matter of chance: we always come back here."

*Though you hardly seem to remember . . . But you already know these garish
signs, these stores, these brown brick walls, these unadorned columns, these windows, these counters, this ocular ceiling painted to look like the sky, this Courtesy
Desk, these hallways, this mural depicting the seasons, this black wishing well fountain, these white and gray tile floors on which you are walking, telling yourself you
do not care, trying to convince yourself you do not care, lying to yourself about
how you do not care, walking to the window to see this water tower in the distance
bearing the mall's logo, a stylized lower case "c" and "h" that together appear to
be the infinity symbol with a superimposed exclamation point, ensuring Chapel
Hill, the friendliest mall of all, would be and go on being, whether you sought it out
or not . . .*

A baseball cracks into a mitt, as the camera now pulls back and reveals Baldy
wearing the same ear protection, Hawaiian shirt not fitting in with what we've
seen of the team earlier, as he transfers the ball to his free hand and throws . . .

    "It was last year. Have I changed so much since then . . . ?"
    Although early in *Last Year at Marienbad*, A tells X she's never been to
Frederiksbad, later M asks where a particular picture of A was taken and she

says Frederiksbad. Did she lie to X? Is she lying to M? Has she forgotten where the picture was taken and therefore answered with any old place name? Or has she only now recalled she was in Frederiksbad upon seeing the picture? I don't know, but I find myself in a similar position, as Baldy stands in a grimy office next to a very tall teenager with blonde hair and round glasses, a thunderous, pulsing sound coming from outside where mammoth diesel engines produce electricity for the mall, as my dad, who looks like a biker, tells me, the camera pulling back revealing a man in dark blue work pants, a light blue grease-stained shirt with a name-badge that reads "Bob," who looks like a biker too, Biker Bob, tells me that when I was a kid, where I wanted to go, above anywhere else, was Chapel Hill.

"I don't think I'm the person you mean. You must be making a mistake."

But I was never a mall rat, so he has to be wrong, the thunderous, pulsing sound from the engines growing more powerful, that couldn't have been me, then the mechanical roar grows quieter and we hear Baldy telling Biker Bob that he and his friend want movie passes, which I do remember, getting cheap tickets to General Cinemas thanks to my dad working for the Chapel Hill Mall power plant, a version of me that makes sense, the film buff, Bob with his permanent sarcastic sneer grabbing the phone, telling the Courtesy Desk he's sending his kid over, except thus far I've been referring to the characters as A, X, and M, since those are their designations in the screenplay, when actually no one in *Last Year at Marienbad* is ever called by any name at all, though I think of them as those letters.

"Or are you pretending not to recognize me?"

Only, I'm not pretending, Biker Bob, incredulous, saying into the phone, What's his *name*?, the tracking on the VHS getting even worse, I just don't remember, as the powerhouse sound begins to change, really *wanting* to go to the mall, Biker Bob, even more sarcastic now, What's my *kid's* name . . . ? I dunno. I'll ask him, my dad telling me he always figured it was because I liked talking to all of the people at Chapel Hill, the people who would go on and on with me, who would somehow forget they were speaking to a child, until they'd look back and see I wasn't who they thought I was, that person, to me, who could not have been me, who was so different, we couldn't possibly both be called . . . Hey, kid, Biker Bob says to Baldy, what's your name? the thunderous engines transforming into the distorted, corrupted, "Maneater," though dissonant now, even strident. Baldy, sincere, confused, obstructed by flipping lines and visual static, answers the question honestly, but looks like he's unsure. And when the very tall teenager and Biker Bob laugh, Baldy looks even less certain.

"You, at least, haven't changed."

A baseball flies through the air toward out-of-focus teammates, though when it looks like it should land in a mitt, the teenagers are gone, the ball bouncing on the cement floor past the diesel engines . . .

"From which there is no escape?"

For a moment, the VHS is clear, the music gone, and Baldy stands in a department store, everyone impeccably dressed, though their clothes don't fit the general '80s milieu, and Baldy's Hawaiian-shirt-with-jeans look doesn't fit in with theirs, which is perhaps why he appears to be hiding from them, ducking behind racks and shelves, freezing next to mannequins, diving under abandoned registers, but even when it's obvious he should be caught, or at least spotted, no one lets on they know he's there, calling to mind the theory that *Last Year at Marienbad* is a kind of adaptation of, or maybe homage to Adolfo Bioy Casares' *The Invention of Morel* (1940). In this novella, the main character, a political prisoner who's escaped Venezuela for the island of Villings, at first thinks he's alone, only to later find there are tourists who might turn him in to the authorities, which leads to the fugitive hiding. One thing he notices about the others is that their clothes, their style is a bit outdated.

"What's become of you in all this time?"

"Nothing, as you see, since I'm still the same."

Intermittently, the visual static returns, so does the music, even more warped than it was before, as Baldy stops the cat and mouse game which, it appears, he wasn't actually playing in the first place, now openly walking in front of people, waving, speaking (inaudibly, since we can't hear him over the persistence of the "Maneater" broadcast from hell), though no one reacts to him, much as the people on Villings don't react to the fugitive even when, no longer able to help himself, he walks right up and starts talking to them.

"I like my freedom."

"Here, for instance?"

"Why not here?"

Baldy, or what we can see of him through the bad tracking, leaves the department store and in his desperation to communicate some message (still blocked out by warbly Hall & Oates), drops all subterfuge, pretense, and tries to talk directly to the people in the mall, tries to talk to anyone, but the Chapel Hill shoppers have a bad habit of vanishing while he's speaking, of reappearing elsewhere, either in the department store (as if they've teleported there), or farther away from Baldy (as if they could walk forever and never arrive at their destinations), much as the fugitive sees two suns and two moons in the sky, sees dead fish in rank aquariums and alive fish in stunning aquariums, sees the tourists in the museum on the island and watches them fade away.

"It's a strange spot."

"You mean: to be free?"

The images from the VHS are losing their coherence, both because of the technological degradation and because, even when you can see what's going on, the only permanent figure is Baldy, crying, unable to get anyone to talk to him, to help him, the mall itself seeming to shift, expand, and contract, perhaps damning our dorky-looking friend to an eternity of creepy saxophone music and spatial flux, with no one able to hear his pleas, meaning no one can tell him what's going on, leaving him completely free in a world where no one thing has any connection to any other thing, much as *The Invention of Morel*, right now, appears to have nothing to do with *Last Year at Marienbad*, even if the novella mentions the place Marienbad early in the going.

"To be free, yes, that in particular."

Though it's almost impossible to make out, Baldy becoming a kind of dark ghost in the center of the screen, there *is* a connection between the Casares novel and the Robbe-Grillet/Resnais film, since the fugitive reveals his existence, as Baldy is finally acknowledged by (of course) the glitchy denizens of the Courtesy Desk, who immediately say, "What's wrong? What's wrong, little boy?" in many simultaneous voices, since the fugitive reveals his existence because he's fallen in love with one of the tourists, named Faustine, and thus he wants to woo her, much as X, who seems to have no connection to anyone at the resort, does the same with A through conversations that frequently feel awkward, forced. But now Baldy is the one impossible to contact, since as the Courtesy Desk employees continue to call him "little boy," it seems like they're actually talking to someone else, much as A in *Marienbad* seems like she's talking to someone other than X, and Faustine in *Morel* to someone other than the fugitive which is, as it turns out, the case since Faustine isn't human, but an image projected by an invention that captures reality and reproduces it in a loop, granting the consciousness of each person immortality, though they are only able to repeat the same thoughts and actions forever (unknown to them), though their bodies are destroyed in the process. If we accept this connection, the fugitive superimposes himself onto Faustine's movie, while X superimposes himself onto A's movie, both constrained by the fact that they can't ask A or Faustine to do anything different than was filmed in the first place, meaning the fugitive and X are working with pre-recorded scenes that they react to, which perhaps explains why Baldy, having superimposed his older self onto his childhood memories, keeps mumbling, "I'm lost, I'm lost," over and over, crying like a little boy, as the visually unstable denizens of the Courtesy Desk shake their heads, and as the VHS finally succumbs to static.

"From which there is no escape."

Baldy, the phantom of the bad tracking, galumphs to the baseball, picks it up, and is immediately seen in perfect clarity. When he looks around, however, not only are his teenage teammates gone, so are the diesel engines. He stands alone in the former Chapel Hill Mall powerhouse, now a storage facility for absence . . .

"And once again, everything is deserted . . ."

The music is gone too, though it was not "Maneater" by Hall & Oates, but a vaporwave remix called "Up Next" by Luxury Elite. If I wanted to continue with the memory cinema conceit I've been using thus far, I could show you Baldy walking through the abandoned mall and you would think it's a prediction of things to come, a prophecy of the at long last deceased Chapel Hill. But much as in *Last Year at Marienbad*, where X and A discuss whether a specific Greco-Roman statue depicts a man who, having spied a danger up ahead, is holding the woman back, or if it depicts a woman who has seen something marvelous and she's now trying to direct the man's attention to it, the scene in the empty mall would be a recollection for me, one calling to mind a time when, after each Thanksgiving my family celebrated at the Brown Derby, we would walk through Chapel Hill, all the stores closed (Black Friday not truly established until 2005), and my sister Stefanie and I would bask in the glow of the coming season.

"I have another game to suggest instead . . ."

But I'm tired of this game because I'm tired of Chapel Hill. It was an important place in my childhood, true, but my dad, who worked at the power plant (and one winter held baseball practice there), was laid off in 1996, the same year I graduated from high school. After that, I had a cynical, ironic view of the mall, to the point that when I walked through it again with him on his 67th birthday, I felt no sadness at the shuttering of Macy's or any number of other stores, and only a bit of a twinge about Sears' impending doom because my dad kept saying, "I can't believe Sears is closing," in a wistful, melancholic way. This same combination of irony and nostalgia can be found in vaporwave, an audio and visual style that uses slowed down and choppy elevator music, smooth jazz, lounge music, and R&B on the aural side, and early Internet imagery, late '90s web design, glitch art, anime, 3-D rendered objects, cyberpunk tropes, Greco-Roman statues, and VHS degradation on the visual side. Vaporwave is even connected to the dead mall/ghost mall phenomenon because of the retro and/or outdated aesthetics (or, as it's stylized in vaporwave, A E S T H E T I C S).

As is obvious, I've been listening to a lot from this genre lately.

"I know a game I always win."

I would argue, while in the past I sit on the patio of a sports bar having just shrugged off my momentary depression and confusion about Chapel Hill, while in the present I sit writing this in my tiki bar of an apartment in Lawrence, Kansas, confused again, that no one song in the vaporwave genre is any good. But when strung together, piece after piece, you begin to believe you're listening to someone's old, very old, very, very old cassette tape collection on a player that needs new batteries, and you can see yourself getting those batteries, putting them into the player, hearing the songs you've always wanted to hear as they were intended to be heard . . . but in actuality you will never get those new batteries because in this eternal ghost mall dimension there are only batteries that are almost dead, and so you listen to the warped, distorted sounds from the speaker, accepting them for the way things are, though occasionally dreaming the true music to yourself, the music you believe you'll hear again someday.

"I can lose, but I always win."

Chapel Hill is a kind of Mall 1.0, without vertiginous stacks of escalators, without mezzanines, without multiple floors, without baroque wings. The brown brick exterior, the predominantly unadorned entrances, the types of stores you'd expect to find anywhere, the horizontal plan that's one straight shot with the slightest cross in the middle like a lowercase t, there could be no mystery there, no, no, not there. At first glance, it seems impossible for anyone, least of all you, for anyone to get lost inside . . . at first glance . . . But, sitting across the street on the patio of that jejune alehouse, ironically detached (or so you thought), as the sun slowly dropped from sight, as darkness activated the spotty illumination around Chapel Hill's parking lot, you could see yourself, past planters that contained and didn't contain plants, past anchors that existed and did not exist, past the bubbling and stagnant wishing well fountain, through Archie's faux-winter wonderland, as the vaporwave "Man-eater" warbled on, unconscious steps directing you down corridors that Dad knew and knows so well, but you not so well, for you were now getting lost, hopelessly lost, forever lost, a phantom eternally wandering through the friendliest (ghost) mall of all, a phantom eternally wandering alone in me.

Bowl-a-Rama

What, bowling? Come on. *Bowling?* It ain't a sport. That's what you tell yourself. I mean, look around. You've got your concession stand with the wall menu still uses those plastic letters you've gotta stick in the slats, about a quarter of them missing. No matter. Place serves up combos of rapidly congealing grease, salt, and sugar. That sound like an *athlete's* diet? There's a bar. A bar! Fully stocked with beers your dad drinks. American Yellows. Can use those to chase the Old Grand Dad, Old Crow, Old Fitzgerald. Unlike in the wide world of sports, "old . . ." well, around here that's a compliment. And it actually means "ancient." Look at the—are we still going with *athletes?* Okay. For now. But look at 'em. On their, sure, why not? *field of play.* Which is hideous casino carpet leading to scuffed to hell linoleum tile and then a bank of benches and chairs made of that '70s two-tone orange and lighter orange plastic (easier to hose off when you slop your coagulated, I guess, *food* on it, when you spill your whiskey and ginger ale on it), all pointed toward the TVs that automatically keep score for you (wouldn't want you to strain yourself now), that show you little cartoons based on how the most recent competitor (*seriously?* wow, just wow) how the most recent *competitor* rolled, everything surrounded by the loudest, most headache-inducing Day-Glo decorations, usually balls and pins, sometimes swooshes and stars. And now see the contenders, the *bowlers.* I'm not saying everyone has to look the same. I'm just saying Olympians they ain't, that is those folks out there on the lanes . . .

Because, as you always tell yourself, this ain't a . . .

The lanes. Something about the lanes makes you wonder. Makes you wonder if maybe bowling is the only sport that discourages you from thinking it's a sport. That's part of the whole deal, see. The people gobbling nachos, chugging brews, swilling whiskey, the screeching little kids rolling balls down the backs of plastic dinosaurs, the bumper alleys, the laughably hideous environs, the odious smells of sweat and grease and stale beer (all strangely coated in talcum powder), the plinking and clanging from the arcade, the unathletic mob, the whole scene, when agglomerated, when Voltron-ed together, forms a kind of kung fu master telling you you've come to the wrong place, there's nothing for you here, what were you thinking? might as well go on back where you came from. Go on, now. Git!

Most of us do. No shame in that. And back where we came from, yeah, we sink a meathook into a mound of chili cheese fries. Suck down a Genny Cream Ale or Busch. Maybe even a Blatz. Chuckle as we watch people scramble around. "Where's Larry? How come every time Larry's up no Larry?" Shrug as we see rollers lumber up to the line, whip the ball down the lane every which way. Marvel as we take in the bowling panorama, since out of the name Bowl-a-Rama, that's the "rama" for us. Wondering where that suffix came from. Learning it got popular in the nineteenth century thanks to diorama. Stuck around just under the radar until Cinerama in the 1950s caused an explosion. After that -aramas or -oramas were slapped on any old thing. Including this here ten-pin entertainment. Later understanding we probably didn't care where "rama" came from in the first place.

Bowl-a-Rama. That's our hangout. Our stomping ground. Our home. No further knowledge is necessary . . .

Except, for those who aren't fooled, who for reasons unknown (perhaps unknowable) decide to take the whole damned thing seriously, who stand firm before the ghostly and disdainful kung fu master made up of the laughable bowling ambience, I'm told for those chosen few (who the jokester doing the choosing is, search me) everything disappears except the lane, the ball, and themselves. From what I hear, as the lane goes, you've gotta figure out how the wood's been oiled—is it a house pattern or sport pattern? The first one is more forgiving and creates a funnel effect toward the pocket, making it easier to roll strikes; the second one, though, is a real bastard, meaning if you miss your mark by just a little bit, the master will send you packing. Then, you have to gauge the *length* of the oil pattern (and here I thought that grease was from all those French fries), taking into account the fact that the longer the pattern, the less your ball will hook. Speaking of the ball, get this!, there are plastic, urethane, reactive resin, and particle bowling balls (this last one must be for *USS Enterprise* crewmembers only), all of which can be fitted with either high mass or low mass weight blocks, all of which can be used to combat different oil patterns or pin setups or both.

But come on! Chaz Dennis, a ten-year-old!, rolled a 300. The United States Bowling Congress even approved the score. How hard could it be?

Ever notice, though, that no one says, "Mozart wrote his first pieces when he was five! How tough could composing classical music be?"

Yeah . . . and anyway, bowling isn't about what you can do once. So whereas a 300 is a perfect *game*, a 900 *series*, or thirty-six strikes in a row, is true perfection. But how you get there, well, that's when the roller comes into play. First, you've got to find the best starting stance. Then, you've got to decide which works better for you, a four- or five-step approach. And let's say you pick the four. All in one fluid motion, you have to use the initial step to push the ball forward, the second step to complete the down-swing while moving your off arm out for balance, the third step to finish the back-swing, and the fourth to bring the ball forward while also crossing your ball-side leg behind your off leg, releasing as you pass your ankle. And once you've determined the length of the oil on the lane, once you've chosen the ball you intend to use, once you've found your mark back at the beginning of league night (meaning, you'll be working with the much tougher sport pattern), you have to go through this ritual exactly the same way thirty-six times in a row to achieve a 900 series. And you must remain focused (so no Pabst or Miller High Life for you). The "Rama" for true bowlers, then, is the avatar of the Hindu god Vishnu. Part human and part deity, Rama brings the passion of a human and the reason of the gods, the self-consciousness of one who has studied (practiced) and the decisive action of an epic hero, the ethics to allow other bowlers to complete their frames and the aesthetics to make it all look so easy (don't worry, even a ten-year-old can do it). Yes, Rama *is* who true bowlers look to, but on the rare occasion when they get close to him (since there have only been thirty-four 900 series ever rolled), they have to come back next week and do it all again. And again. And again. The bodily mastery and intense concentration needed for twelve strikes, for twenty-four strikes, for thirty-six strikes then has to be repeated for an entire *season*.

Who could do that?

What *mortal* could do that?

The answer is: no mortal.

It's enough to make you want a beer. Any kind will do.

One ice-cold American Yellow . . .

And, buddy, why not? Why *the hell* not? Come on! It's not the time to talk about avatars or whatever. This, *this* is entertainment. Amusement. Look at the place. Just look at it. Are you getting an *athletic excellence* vibe here? You know why? Because, say it with me now, "Bowling. Is not. A sport." Don't you feel better? So drink that beer. More fries will be on the way. And if you can find a Larry, probably by the time you get back he'll be up.

Noir Girl

(An Essay in Two Takes)

When I first laid eyes on her, I called her Noir Girl . . .
And that's exactly what she became.

First Take: Film Noir at the Crystal Lounge

No one plans on going to the Crystal Lounge, everyone just ends up there. A dive like that, people treat it as if the place didn't have any doors. The folks on the outside are left to wonder how you get sucked in, how you could let that happen to yourself, it's your own fault, pal, you *knew* the consequences . . . while figuring the people on the inside don't worry about getting out. Leave? And go where, exactly? There's someplace else? First I've heard about it.

Now the ones who *don't* become regulars, after they disappear inside the Crystal for a night, later recount stories that sound like a fevered amalgam of Poe and Hammett, Lovecraft and Chandler, nightmares and false awakenings they couldn't snap out of, knowing none of it could've been real, but for all that it continued on, an unabashed, corporeal hallucination, a dreamscape not the least bit interested in verisimilitude, the red and black bar, the red and black carpet, the red and black stools and chairs, the walls red because of the red lights, the sometimes horrific, sometimes (and this was creepier) melodic singing, the sordid deals, the lascivious gyrating, the sleaze, the relentless gambling on absolutely anything (the cacophony of the slot machines will be with me always), the faces so heavily made up they looked like masks, everyone and everything maybe inspired by those dark, German silent films . . . Come on, man, come *on*, where in the *world* did you go?

The answer's always the same.

The commercial even has a word for it: Crystalized.

When it all went wrong between me and her, afterwards, having unconsciously found the familiar, I'd never felt more Crystalized in my life . . .

※

"Will I ever see you again?"

"Probably. I'm in this bar almost every night."

※

I never intended to become a regular at the Crystal because I didn't intend to stay in Montana that long. Actually, I thought I was moving on soon. Very soon. So when I saw her sitting there by herself, I pegged her for a visitor like me. Someone who'd paused on their journey. Someone who'd taken a sidetrek. Someone who was definitely headed elsewhere, wherever that might be. Until then, let's have fun and check out the locals.

For people who don't frequent bars, it's probably difficult to understand the attraction. Here you are, sitting in a room, normally a rather tawdry room, with nothing to do but drink. There may be televisions and games of some sort, but the people who are there for the televisions, who are there for the games are a different breed, chasing a different dream. The true regular is after this: the illusion of being someone. Because if you're someone, then *something* should happen to you, something has to happen already, it just has to. In the old, hard-boiled novels, there's often a point where the characters and even the readers ask, "How could it come to this?" The answer's simple: they were bored. They didn't want a normal life. They wanted something else. They wanted *something* to happen.

Sitting at the bar, the lovers, the fighters, the comedians, the politicos, the amateur philosophers, the mystics, the conspiracy theorists, and all the other liars tell their stories to themselves and anyone else who'll listen, each one ending, someday, with a grand departure—the Crystal Lounge? are you kidding? have you seen it? of course I left . . . they're probably still talking about me down there, though—going on to something greater (even if that "greater" is fantastically sordid), leaving the broken and bereft clientele like a god's avatar who can now only be experienced through tall tales that the regulars spin when they grow tired of their own: have you ever heard about . . . you haven't? oboy. Here. We. Go . . .

None of these stories ever come true. None of them come true, and yet somehow they exist in this place . . . Of course, you *can* leave, thinking you've finally found that something or someone who'll propel you beyond the bar. You can even swear never to return. Won't matter to us. Just words. You can't stay away. Your *dreams* live here. So we know you'll be back. And we'll see you again soon. Real soon.

That's why the ones who end up marked by the taint of the Crystal, that hand-stamp never quite washing away even after hard scrubbing, coarse soap, bleach for Chrissakes, won't it ever come off?! well you can see the neon sign's red, yellow, and green in their eyes. It beckons to them wherever they are.

It beckons to me now. So I'll pretend to be a regular:

Walking in, passing that Big Lug the Doorman with a salute, the Gorgeous Cocktail Waitress with a wave, the Bearded Bartender unconsciously reaching for my preferred poison, the ironically dim atmosphere of the Crystal Lounge, deep shadows everywhere, its own tenebrous ecosystem that sustains and destroys us all, and then, time slowing down, there, right over there, dark and mysterious, exhaling seductively, the smoke spiraling in, how could that be?, glowing vortices that create a swirling maze in the air, the clew for which doesn't get you out, no no no, it ensures you'll remain lost, lost forever, and I'd happily get lost forever in that labyrinth if it meant I was lost with . . . yes, there, at the end of the bar, cigarette in hand, it's her . . .

Only, it doesn't work like that. She just appeared next to me at some point. Sure, Stillson, a friend of mine, used to wear a BAN NON-SMOKING T-shirt. But it wasn't banned. Instead, everyone quit. Even *he* quit. So now smoky barrooms can only be visited in our dreams. Typical . . .

That night was anything but typical, though. I was optimistic. And nothing good *ever* comes of optimism.

"Did my name come up while I was gone?"

"Yes."

"*You*? You don't even *know* my name."

"True. That's true. But your name came up just the same."

❧

I couldn't help myself. I thought I'd found a way out. The interview, the job, the city. At the time, I thought I'd knocked the first out of the park, that the second was as good as mine, and that the third would soon be my home, a home where I'd belong... unlike Billings. Unlike Montana. Normally, I'm protected from delusions like these by an extreme cynicism, a darkness I refuse to see as negative. To me it's just realistic. But that evening, the world was so full of light, I was dazzled...

And like an emissary from this new, refulgent world, there she sat by herself, two barstools away.

Although brimming with confidence, I lacked something much more important: experience. I'm clueless when it comes to picking up . . . anyone. What are the mechanics? How does it happen? I don't know. Say what you want about cheesy lines, they work far better and more frequently than frustrated and confused silence. Don't get me wrong, I talk to people in bars all the time. But that's just talk. And contrary to what people seem to believe, that sort of exchange leads to drinking buddies, good pals, and nothing else. The Ladies' Man behind me, he knows what to say, and he knows how to say it in such a way that the women chase after him. I don't have that skill, so normally I'd rationalize: a girl that attractive, her husband, boyfriend, or posse of knockouts will be along soon enough, and I can go ahead and fade into the background.

Only that didn't happen. She remained alone. And I sat there trying to figure out what character I was in this story. If I knew that, I'd know what to say. But then the Ladies' Man crashed into me, far drunker than I'd ever seen him before, saying:

"Andy, Andy, Annnnndy, are you, are you gonna . . . sing, Andy?"

I said: "Of course I am, already put my request in," turning to her, seeing a possible opening, "and what are *you* gonna sing?" Instantly she slid down the two barstools, replying that she didn't sing, but that she was hanging out with me now. Turning around, I saw that the Ladies' Man had drunkenly wandered away, that no one was around me and her, and I began to believe that this bright new world was less prescribed than the old dark one, that nobody was following their character arcs anymore.

I was wrong.

"I think you come here too much."

"I do?"

"I see you in this bar all the time."

"It's a coincidence. I just happen to be here when you come in."

"There are no coincidences."

"Well, I see you in here all the time too."

"I know. It's because I come here too much."

"What a coincidence. So do I."

"The jobs I've had could be done by a hamster on a wheel," she said, and what could I do? All I could see was . . .

There should be a service called Eclipse for people like me. Here's how it'd work: after you sign up, their agents observe your life. Nothing intrusive. You wouldn't even know they're there. Until things started to get too bright. Then, then they'd swing by, remind you who you are, what your place is in the universe, just a little realignment, don't worry about it, buddy, even the best of us get taken in. If that doesn't work, they'd seed clouds to block out the sun, dim all the lights (swapping out your bulbs for half the wattage), tint your windows and windshield, even your contacts or glasses — they would, for a nominal fee, reinstall all of the shadows of the world, making them darker, darker, so much darker than they were before, obscuring that refulgence you'd gotten to believing in, and then you'd remember why you pay the fine folks over at Eclipse, why you've recommended them, without reservation, to each and every one of your friends.

But there is no Eclipse, so after various nonstarters, and a moment where I thought she had nothing to say about anything, when I asked where she worked, she said: "The jobs I've had could be done by a hamster on a wheel. It's true. Now I know, to be someone, to really *do* something, I have to leave, I have to go somewhere else. Europe, Asia . . . Look, I always knew there would be things missing from my life. Things like wealth, fame, beauty . . ."

"Beauty? But you have to know you're very . . ."

"Oh, *I* know . . ."

I'm not sure what I expected. A hookup? A new kind of drinking buddy? A reset on my entire social life up to that point? What I do know is that it felt like Montana, Billings, the Crystal Lounge were all fading into the distance, can't even see them in my rearview mirror anymore, while she and I were moving on. It seemed somehow criminal. Like we were planning a heist, one big score that'd take care of everything. Ridiculous? Sure. But that's how it felt.

It was so loud in the bar, we had to sit close together to hear each other, all accidental grazes dealt with by polite retreats from both sides. After we connected through our history of lousy jobs, she told me her life story—she told me that she was adopted, that her foster family was very religious (which she did not like, even though she believed in God), that to rebel she teamed up with the kids at school who sold pot, that she took the fall for one of her friends, that she ended up in a group home (instead of going to juvie) where she met so many interesting people that now she goes to bars for the same experience, and that after she finished high school, she had to wait until she was an independent in order to go to college, so she became a grinder at the contemporary mill: customer service.

Maybe her story reminded me of those old, hard-boiled novels again (femme fatales struggling to get by, not wanting a *normal* life). Maybe I was excited because for the first time ever I actually hit it off with a girl I met at a bar. Whatever the reason, the light burned with an unsustainable intensity. If only the agents from Eclipse had been there to say, "You didn't do so hot at that interview. You're not getting the job. You aren't moving to that city. As for this girl . . . come on. We'll buy you a drink." Then they'd direct me to a table in a dark, dark corner (don't even remember this table or this corner being here). They'd remind me who I was. They'd remind me about my place in the universe. And cloaked in that shadow, my mindset would be realigned.

No such luck. Instead, having covered the past in the Crystal Lounge, I felt we needed to cover the future somewhere else (not realizing our relationship could only exist in one place).

As we left, I said: "You're a fabulous mystery."

She said: "You're a mystery too."

A mystery. Exactly what I needed, exactly what I wanted to be . . . Yeah, right there, I thought I'd found that someone, that someone who'd propel me beyond the bar, I thought one of the stories I'd been telling myself was finally coming true, I thought I'd never return. If I'd been listening (no one ever listens), I could've heard an eerie voice say:

You'll be back.

"Can you forget what we were talking about last time?"

"I can if you want me to."

"I want you to."

"Then it's forgotten."

"Well, you have the mountains." That's what everyone says . . . when you tell them you live in Montana, when you tell them it's not working out. "Well . . . you have the mountains." A constant refrain. As if whatever ailed you, whatever was bothering you, whatever troubles you might have could be cured just by looking at those ancient masses of rock. Back in the Midwest, it's the opposite. If you have anything good to say, if you've had any positive experiences there, if you found things you didn't expect to find, it won't matter, just keep it all to yourself, buddy, because if you don't, well, whoever you're talking to will pause . . . and then deliver this immortal line: "I don't know, it's just so flat." Any heights you might've built up in your mind will instantly be hammered down to pancakes flaccidly littering the landscape for as far as the eye can see.

I sat looking for those mountains, looking forlorn, right there in the Crystal Lounge. No doors. No windows. There's somewhere else? First I've heard of it. When the Gorgeous Cocktail Waitress saw me, she asked what was wrong, what happened. I wanted to tell her, but I felt that I lacked the language, the vocabulary having not yet been established that could accurately explain what'd occurred, the genre undefined. I wanted to tell her, but none of it seemed real, having taken place . . . elsewhere. And I couldn't imagine there was an elsewhere. I was a regular. There was only here.

I turned to another part of the bar, a part where my fabulous mystery and I had hung out before, before, before it was me, despondent, all by my lonesome, surrounded by people, sure, but none of them the one I was looking for, hoping for, yearning for (yeah, it was that bad) on Valentine's Day. Later on she'd say, "You were depressed on VD Day? *VD* Day?!" mocking, laughing, and I didn't blame her. Hell, I even joined in. But in that moment, alienated from everyone, me and my whiskey, the bar's red lights a constant reminder of that horrid holiday, a holiday I'd ignored without a second thought for thirty-seven years, I felt the vacuum of the West, the nothingness that encircles Billings extending out for hundreds of miles in every direction, and each odometer click registered on an internal gauge I'd never used before, that I'd never even known about before, telling me just how alone I was . . .

Maybe, maybe if I'd found those mountains everyone else believed in, I would've hardened, solidified, I would've been whole again. But this is Billings we're talking about. There aren't any mountains. There *are* the Rimrocks to the north. Otherwise, it's flat. Like the Midwest. And anyway, staring at big, dumb heaps of rock doesn't make you any calmer, any wiser. Nature doesn't work like that. Not for me. So I looked up, wishing, hoping, yearning, and I scanned the crowd, and there, as if in answer to my unspoken plea, there she was . . . so amazed I had to ask the Bartender, "Is that . . . is that her?"

Entranced, I walked over and joined the one I'd been looking for, hoping for. I joined her so we could observe a holiday I'd somehow forgotten about my entire life. In a manner of speaking, this was my first. We needed to do something to commemorate the occasion, we needed to celebrate. And we did. There, at the Crystal Lounge, we celebrated. And why not? It was Valentine's Day.

When we parted, I watched her walk until I couldn't see her anymore, up Broadway, past the shops and offices of downtown Billings, and into the night. Later, after our last meeting, I'd stare up the street and remember, wishing our story had gone on and on. But it didn't. And I never saw her again.

Second Take: Neo-Noir at the Babcock Theatre

As I watched Noir Girl walk away for the last time, I finally knew . . . I finally knew what role I was playing. It was a role I'd played before all too often. It was a role I was sick of—the Social Misfit. I would've exchanged it for almost any other. But in that moment, a fury of confusion having just subsided, I was content . . .

On the screen: *A man drops a cigarette into gasoline; a ship docked at a pier explodes.*

... I was content because I knew ...

Or, as it turns out, I thought I knew ...

From the outside, the Babcock Theatre looks like it'd have a constant noir marathon playing there because it looks like the sort of place that'd appear in a noir film: big old marquee, Babcock coolly burning in blue neon script, the sign hinged at a point that pulses red bottom to top, luring your eyes ever upward where yellow and white swooshes glow, the whole shebang either a bright, blaring beacon beckoning you to the fantasy world inside, or a self-conscious nostalgia machine that seduces you, convincing you to go ahead, indulge in that hankering you have for movies ... well, when it's lit. And it isn't lit very often. What do you expect? This is Billings. So that noir marathon, yeah, it isn't exactly continuous. More continual.

The screen says: *"The explanation is never that complicated. It's always simple."*

Stillson says: *"Things like this just don't happen."*

Back in Chicago, where I got my Ph.D., I was known as the noir guy. It was one of the fields I was studying and similar themes came up in my fiction. So when I joined a bunch of folks to see improv comedy at the iO Theatre and one of the troupes performed a skit about detective stories, everybody I knew looked over at me like I had something to do with it. I mean, come on. I hadn't done a goddamned thing.

Always the Social Misfit.

None of the strengths, all of the weaknesses.

Because of my perpetual role I was clueless, so I asked my friend, the Hookup Artist, for some advice. I told her I was going out with Noir Girl, but unlike the past two times, when we ran into each other at the Crystal Lounge, this time, well, I didn't know if it was a date, or if we were just friends, or ... or what. The Hookup Artist, as I expected, knew what to do. She said that uncertainty was normal. She said that even she had been uncertain from time to time (hard to believe, maybe a placation device). She said that since Noir Girl and I enjoyed hanging out in bars, on this occasion I was to invite her to another bar. Something different. A change of venue. I was to buy Noir Girl one drink and only one drink. Something nice. A friend could do that. It wasn't intrusive. Under no circumstances was I to recommend dinner. Dinner might happen sometime in the future, but not on this night. This night was to be drinks at a different, preferably nicer bar. From there, if the uncertainty resolved itself, accept the resolution. If the uncertainty didn't resolve, return for further instructions. I thought this was a solid plan mostly because it wasn't my own. Whatever I came up with certainly would've failed.

The screen says: *"Did you put that together yourself, Einstein? What, do you got a team of monkeys working around the clock?"*

The cadet says: *"Don't try to make this make sense."*

I have a theory on where this sunny disposition of mine comes from. At least in part. One summer, when I was a kid, it was learned that a basic cable station planned to play every single Humphrey Bogart flick there ever was. Right there on TV. And if someone were to record these films, then that bright boy would own Bogie's lifework. Wouldn't cost him a dime. All he'd have to do is make sure the commercials were . . . taken care of, so to speak. Anybody could do it really. Should he be successful, and should he hand this merchandise off to the right people, the bosses would look favorably on that bright boy. Know of anyone who'd be interested?

There wasn't actually a choice. The equipment for the job was a stack of videotapes, a silver VHS, and a corded (not cordless) remote control. In the beginning, it seemed so simple. The commercials come on, hit PAUSE. The commercials end, hit PAUSE again. That way the people who watched the movies in the future could do so uninterrupted, could even think they were getting away with something. I know a guy. He took care of everything. Don't worry about it. He's the best.

He's the best.

That's what I told myself.

But then I noticed something—there were no warnings. The commercials just . . . began . . . and the movie just . . . resumed. Any fade out or cut *could* mean it was time to hit PAUSE, or it could mean nothing at all. At first, I was unfazed. I was the best. With each darkening screen, though, I became less sure. Whereas before I eliminated advertisements with confidence, now my remote finger became itchy. I tried to pay closer attention to the movies, tried to figure out how long the film normally ran before the sponsors broke in, tried to predict when we'd return to that glorious black-and-white, tried to guess when it was time to PAUSE. I couldn't do it anymore. I'd lost my nerve. I was doomed to fail. And then, it got worse.

As I became more and more agitated, I accidentally pulled the remote's cord out of its connector. Not all the way out. That would've been an easy fix. Just enough to make me powerless against the oncoming tide of advertisements without knowing why. Now, it didn't matter when or even if I pressed the button. Nothing happened. A madman, I continued to try, thinking it'd work again, it *had* to work again, what was going on here?! And as each commercial was recorded onto the tape, that permanent record of my failure, I knew the bosses would have no choice, we gave him every opportunity, and maybe the FBI would receive an anonymous tip, find me surrounded by pirated Bogart films, *it's not what you think!*, or maybe someone, somewhere holding his own remote would hit PAUSE on my life . . . and it would never resume.

Only, in the end, there was no hell to pay. And I don't remember ever seeing those tapes again. I certainly don't remember anyone watching them. Instead, it appears, the point of that job wasn't the job itself, it was the outlook the job instilled in me. No matter what, I couldn't understand those movies. I was far too young. But the situation taught me most everything I needed to know about paranoia and pessimism, while the images that were etched onto my impressionable brain filled in the gaps. So when I met Noir Girl, the nickname I'd give her came to mind immediately, and I felt right at home.

Inside, the Babcock looks like the movie palaces of the past . . . I figure. Or, at least, when I think of movie palaces of the past, I imagine its layout: red velvet seats, the aisles, the floor of the lobby, the stairs up to the balcony covered in red carpet that's heavily padded underneath, the walls decorated with baroque designs difficult to remember when you're elsewhere, but absolutely familiar when you're there. If you should find yourself lost in this lush luxuriousness, never fear, for certainly you can't miss the ushers in their red and black toy soldier uniforms with the round hats. Of course, unlike at the local megaplexes, the screen stands on a stage, the proscenium arch capped by an ornate, golden sculpture depicting fierce, curling clouds, enticing you to look up even higher at what is often a depiction of the night sky. There've been vaguely similar theatres in all the places I've lived, each one, at some point, having undergone an extensive remodel, ensuring it looked exactly the way it did in the good old days, though all the materials have been replaced by newer materials, all the technology replaced by more advanced technology, a façade that's both nostalgic and completely ahistorical. And yet, before the renovations, the Babcock had briefly been a boxing venue. Nothing more film noir than fixed fights; nothing more neo-noir than a movie palace that once housed a squared circle now showing a noir marathon.

The screen says: *"I'm sure you've heard many tall tales."*

The Cat says: *"You have to be doing something to make this happen."*

The fix was in. Well, almost. Back in Chicago, everyone looked at me when the gumshoe skit ended. It hadn't been very good, and I felt like they were blaming me. *You did this to us. You.* I mean, yeah, sure, I had been the one who shouted, "Detectives!" when the troupe called for a theme, but I only volunteered because this was like the fifth group up and by that time no one in the audience was interested in participating anymore. Consequently, when the actors asked, at first there was dead silence, a silence that ratcheted the tension up higher and higher each second, a silence that seemed indestructible . . . until my voice finally murdered it . . . So maybe, maybe the folks I was hanging out with weren't blaming me. Maybe their collective look was one of sympathy. *You almost got what you wanted, but not quite.*

The screen says: *"It's because you're stupid. It's because you're a cripple."*

The gambler says: *"I've seen a lot of weird things happen. A year from now, maybe in an airport, O'Hare even, you'll run into her and she'll say, 'Oh, man, do you remember that bizarre night we went out? Well, lemme tell you what happened . . .'"*

Noir Girl, she understood where I was coming from. We met at a bar called TEN, its sign a clock with the number 10 at every position on the face, and she got it. "I always ask for a fork," she said when I told her I can't use chopsticks. "I mean, come on. I'm an American . . . They even have those kiddie chopsticks with the rubber band for slow people like us," she made an awkward pincer with her fingers, "but I still always ask for the fork."

It was a good line and secretly I thanked her for it. I'd been nervous because I couldn't dissuade her from dinner. What I really wanted to do was follow the Hookup Artist's plan exactly as laid out, but Noir Girl wasn't interested. Who could blame her? She didn't even know there was a plan. Thinking about this moment, though, when she jokingly mocked us for being slow, when she relaxed me, when she made me feel like we were there together, instead of accidentally adjacent (an accident that'd be fixed right quick, too), I wish I could tell you more about her, much more than I have, but my lawyer says no. "Don't give any identifying facts, and don't use any names. That's your free legal advice." And so, sadly, she must remain a shadow, an unknown.

The screen says: *"It all makes sense when you look at it right. You gotta like stand back from it, you know?"*

The mystic says: *"You have been gifted one short story."*

But then maybe my lawyer, by forcing me to work with an unknown, gave me a gift. Unknowns have always been interesting to me. An editor described my first book this way: "[Farkas] effs the ineffable." Maybe Quentin Tarantino's to blame . . .

The way I remember it, my friend Red introduced everyone at Stow-Munroe Falls High School to *Pulp Fiction* (1994), a film that follows the movements of a mysterious, glowing briefcase; the contents are never revealed. Maybe, if I'd been a teenager in the '50s, I would've been more interested in *solved* mysteries, since *Kiss Me Deadly* (1955) uses the same trick, but by the end there's no question what's inside. Instead, we had long discussions over what that briefcase held, going back to the movie itself again and again, searching for the missing clue that'd finally lead to the solution. Along the way, we picked up the characters' speech patterns, their vocabulary, their idioms, their lines, *English, motherfucker, do you speak it?*, well, only as a second language. Because now we spoke in *Pulp Fiction*. For a time, the screenplay became our sacred text and the reciting of it our ritual . . .

Nobody had it worse than Red. At one point, he tells me, he was even in danger of losing his identity. And so, for his own good (according to him), Red was kidnapped, taken to a re-education camp where no one acknowledged the existence of *Reservoir Dogs* (1992), let alone any other Tarantino film, and there he was taught to be himself again. This was after he saw *Pulp Fiction* twenty-three times at the theatre; this was after he bought the Japanese laser disc so he could have a copy of the film before anyone else (and who knows how many times he watched that). Those of us who were close to him knew he'd hit rock bottom when he couldn't form thoughts unless those thoughts could be expressed via *Pulp Fiction*, when he couldn't respond to someone except through a line from the movie. And yet even for Red, a guy who almost became the film, who was almost consumed by the film, a guy who may know more about it than either Tarantino or Roger Avary or both combined, the contents of the briefcase remain unknown. As for me, thanks in part to *Pulp Fiction*'s influence, I continue on . . . trying to eff the ineffable.

❦

Beneath the Babcock Theatre . . . what did I expect to find there? Ancient Vaudeville props? Old movie posters? An entrance into a filmic underworld where a colony of movie buffs reenacted their favorite pictures? I can't say. But when I saw the Babcock for the first time, I immediately understood that I had to explore every square inch of it, that this exploration had to take place at night, and that I just had to find something, something that couldn't be named beforehand, something that'd certainly be mind-bending afterwards . . . Afterwards . . . Yeah, afterwards, thanks to my investigation, I would know. I would know. And that's the true difference between film noir and neo-noir—film noir never knew what it was (the flicks originally categorized as thrillers, police procedurals, detective films, gangster pictures, suspense, etc.), while neo-noir, neo-noir always did.

As you'll see, I didn't actually know what'd happened with Noir Girl. Instead, I just thought I went on a bad date (though I knew pretty quickly it wasn't really a date at all). And so, the next morning, or, actually, the next afternoon, I sat in my apartment with a hangover, talking on the phone with friends of mine about the night before. The story, at that time, much like my story about exploring the Babcock's basement, wasn't, in my opinion, very interesting. Feeling bad for myself, I told it anyway. I said that after the auspicious beginning at TEN, things changed dramatically. She spent the majority of the night either in the bathroom or texting. Occasionally, she'd look up from her phone, scan the restaurant or bar behind me, and laugh. When I asked what was going on, she'd say, "Oh, nothing." Later, she asked me what my plans were for the night, as if we hadn't planned on doing what we were doing, as if we'd run into each other by chance. Things only got worse from there. Whereas before she mostly ignored me, as the evening wore on, I grew more and more transparent, fading away into nothingness.

The screen says: *"It didn't make sense that I'd be there . . . but there I was."*

The gambler says: *"Now I want you to go on a date with a real girl. This one, in my opinion, she doesn't count as real."*

I continued to believe that I'd find something mind-bending in the Babcock, specifically in the basement of the Babcock, even once I'd descended and found . . . nothing. Getting down there was easy, and that should've tipped me off; it didn't. For some reason. The space was bigger than I figured, sure. The rooms were dark, each one containing a motion-activated light, and while my eyes adjusted to that radiant explosion, every single time I thought, "This will be the one." No dice. Instead, I saw some broken down appliances, an old couch, and a lot of busted cement. Junk. Walking back up the stairs, however, I realized I had been right—my investigation led to knowing; I had come to know I was a fool.

The screen says: *"Back when I was picking beans in Guatemala, we used to make fresh coffee, right off the trees I mean. That was good. This is shit, but, hey, I'm in a police station."*

The Gorgeous Cocktail Waitress says: *"When you hear that word, you immediately think of two things."*

A fool. As it turns out, although I'm a doctor of language, I didn't know the legal definitions of two words. I had their general meanings down pat, sure, but that's all. And so, sitting there at the third venue we visited that night (a swanky cocktail bar), desperate to slough off my Social Misfit costume that I felt creeping up my body for anything else, I started mentioning things we'd talked about on Valentine's Day in an attempt to recapture what we had at the Crystal. That's when she slowly turned toward me (the now extremely visible man), narrowed her eyes, and said:

"Are you a narc?"

My lawyer says: *"I've known many a narc, and you, my friend, don't resemble them in any way. But if she were a call girl, she would have thought you were [a narc] because you weren't soliciting her. Cops have to let them make the first move. I guess the moral of the story is, 'It makes you seem untrustworthy not to offer random women money for sex.' But that moral might have limited application."*

The screen says: *"Where's your head?"*

My mind was melting. I told her I was who I said I was: an Assistant Professor of Creative Writing at Rocky Mountain College. I had told her before, but it sounded strangely suspicious to me, so I said she could go up whenever she wanted and ask the secretaries and administrators and other professors and instructors (listing specific people I knew). I might've even said that she could hangout on campus and snag random students and ask *them*. I told her all of the schools that I went to, even the undergrad institution I attended for a single semester. I told her all the writers I've worked with, both the ones who were my teachers and the ones who were my peers. I might've even started listing off the various journals where I've published work. I definitely offered to give her a copy of my book. And I said all of this because I thought she had just accused me of being an undercover narcotics officer.

It wasn't until the next day that The Oil & Water King set me straight: a narc was also an undercover vice cop. Somehow, I hadn't known. And right then I felt more invisible than I had the entire night before.

The Romanian says: *"Now that you know she's a call girl, you can do whatever you want to with her. Which is what call girls are for."*

The screen says: *"The greatest trick the devil ever pulled was convincing the world he didn't exist."*

I hadn't always thought ill of invisibility. From eighth to tenth grade, I lived a daily nightmare that affects me to this very day. Other people I knew who experienced the same torture fantasized about being the dominant ones. Not me. I dreamed of vanishing; I dreamed of Keyser Söze. So whereas *Pulp Fiction* exerted a massive force on my friends, even becoming a black hole that almost tore Red apart, my own obsession was *The Usual Suspects* (1995). Much like Tarantino and Avary's glowing briefcase, Bryan Singer and Christopher McQuarrie's Keyser Söze is an unsolvable mystery. At different points in the film, he could be anyone or no one. And even after the dramatic reveal that is the movie's conclusion, it still isn't clear whether this Hungarian (or Turkish or maybe German) arch-villain is real, or if he's just a spook story. Don't get me wrong, it wasn't the violence or the crime that attracted me to Keyser Söze, that persuaded me to use his handle at any event where inputting a name was required. It was the fact that he could influence so much without being there physically. Later, I'd come to realize only writing would allow me to emulate this ethereal gangster. By becoming an author, I could finally be Keyser Söze.

The screen says: *"A rumor's not a rumor that doesn't die."*

The playboy says: *"In fact, it is your complete lack of game that makes you a Jedi and endears you to barkeeps and prostitutional types."*

I didn't feel like a mastermind at that time, no. I felt more like a detective who realizes he's gotten everything wrong. A common trope. But the dramatic revelations weren't over quite yet . . .

Thanks to The Oil & Water King, my depression (and my hangover) evaporated. Here I had called her Noir Girl and now it seemed like I was in a noir. I immediately wanted to get in touch with her, to tell her I had no intention of bringing the curtain down on her operation, that whatever she did was just fine with me, but I had no idea how to go about it. In the meantime, I called my friend Thursday to tell her the story, realizing that this time the tone would be different. After all, it was no longer film noir; it was neo-noir.

I told Thursday: the second legal word I didn't know? *Emancipated.* Before, in my opinion, *emancipated* and *emancipation* were only to be used in connection with freeing the slaves during the Civil War. That's it. Nothing else. I was wrong. But Noir Girl didn't use the word *emancipated.* Instead, she used a word not present either in legalese or common usage: *unemancipated.* She told me that after getting busted for selling marijuana, she ended up in a group home in Montana (though she was not from Montana). She told me that because she was *unemancipated,* she was able to stay in the group home, instead of returning to her foster family in the state she's actually from.

Thursday informed me that nothing about this story was true. Thursday informed me that in order to be *emancipated,* a minor has to prove to a judge that he or she can live without their parents (normally because of a hostile or otherwise dangerous environment). Thursday informed me that you have to know the right word in order to convince the judge. Thursday informed me that once a minor is *emancipated,* he or she becomes a ward of the state, meaning you can't just choose some other state to go live in. Thursday informed me, referencing *narc* and *unemancipated,* that I'd certainly chosen some . . . interesting? sure, why not, let's go with *interesting* people to hang out with in Montana.

On the screen: *A coffee cup falls to the floor over and over from many different angles.*

Stillson says: *"Things like this just don't happen. People date and it either goes well or it doesn't. People have sex, and maybe there's a pregnancy scare or a disease scare, or maybe there isn't and they keep meeting up for a while, and then it's over. No one goes on a date with a secret prostitute who previously delivered an elaborate lie for no reason over the course of two nights and who then disappears . . . Except you. I've decided—you're a realist. It's just the things that happen to you don't happen to anyone else, so everyone thinks your writing is weird."*

In Chicago, I gave a sly smile and a nod. My friends were looking at me, so I had to do *something.* The sleuth skit, well, yeah, it wasn't very good. Except, that is, for the conclusion. After a rather bumbling, not particularly funny take on the genre, the last scene focused on two characters talking about how they preferred older detective stories to the newer ones. The older ones, they said, had order, had solutions, had closure, whereas the newer ones were chaotic, the solutions didn't matter, "And then," one of the characters said, "they just . . ." The lights on the stage went out. Everyone immediately turned in my direction, their eyes accusing me of somehow making this happen, of somehow transforming this routine into one of my own stories. There was absolute silence, as if I would deliver an acceptable explanation. What could I say? I mean, come on. I hadn't done a goddamned thing!

But I pretended like I did.

The screen says: *"You think a guy like that comes this close to getting caught and sticks his head out?"*

Walking up the stairs from the basement, I turn at the main floor, open the door that says Babcock Apartments. I keep going up, thinking about all the times I've told this story. I think about the fact that in the written version I can't use Noir Girl's real name, so I've decided I won't use anyone's real name (except my own). Instead, I'll use generic types and slightly misleading descriptions. Stillson only sort of works with wrenches. The Romanian, she isn't actually Romanian. My lawyer isn't my lawyer, he's just *a* lawyer who said I could call him "my lawyer" to impress people at bars. Hell, the only reason there's a continual film noir/neo-noir festival showing in the Babcock Theatre is because I live in the same building, so the festival plays on my TV.

What I think about most, though, is how I feel when I tell the story. The first few times, before The Oil & Water King and Thursday educated me, I was the same as the character I was portraying. Not anymore. Now, it feels like a ruse, it feels like I did something to make this happen, it feels like I found a way to transform my life into a noir, and even though I had to play the dupe, being my only opportunity, I grabbed it.

The screen says: *"After that . . . my guess is you'll never hear from him again."*

I sit down at my desk and write:

"Noir Girl and the Social Misfit walk out of the Crystal Lounge, the Social Misfit sporting a bit of a limp, his foot having fallen asleep while sitting at the bar.

"'You're a fabulous mystery,' he says."

"'You're a mystery too,' she says."

"They continue up Broadway until Skypoint looms overhead, where plans are made to contact each other soon. And then, without touching, they say goodnight. Noir Girl struts past the shops and offices of downtown Billings, while the Social Misfit, who can't help himself, watches her fade into the night.

Alone now, the Social Misfit makes his way down 2nd Avenue toward the home of the continual film noir/neo-noir festival, toward the Babcock Theatre, still limping at first, but growing more sure-footed with each step. Once more, however, he turns back, as if marveling at what he's made happen, what he's making happen, before opening the door, and disappearing inside."

The screen says: *"And like that . . . he's gone."*

ACKNOWLEDGMENTS

The following essays originally appeared in this or some other form in the following journals:

"The Great Indoorsman" in *Heavy Feather Review* (February 2019).
"Wait Here?" in *3:AM Magazine* (June 2019).
"A Filk Tale" (under the title "Filk") in *The Iowa Review* 49.1 (Spring 2019).
"Pool Hall Legend" in *decomP magazinE* (September 2019).
"Somewhere Better Than This Place" in *The Florida Review* 37.1 (Summer 2012). This piece was a Notable Essay in *Best American Essays 2013*.
"Time Stands Still When You're Havin' Fun" in *Always Crashing* (September 2019). This piece was nominated for a Pushcart Prize and for *Best of the Net 2020*.
"Still Life with Alarm Clocks" in *Big Muddy* 20 (Winter 2020).
"When Hamburger Station Is Busy" in *Willow Springs* 88 (Fall 2021).
"Bowl-a-Rama" in *Vol. 1 Brooklyn* (October 2020).
"Noir Girl" in *North American Review* 303.1 (Winter 2018). This piece was nominated for a Pushcart Prize.

Thank you to Courtney Ochsner and the University of Nebraska Press for letting the word of the Indoors ring out across the land (and then to scurry back inside where it's most comfortable).

Thank you to Lily Hoang for her insight.

Thank you to my students and colleagues at Washburn University.

Thank you to David Giffels (who read a different book of my essays when he was a reporter for the *Akron Beacon Journal* and I contacted him out of the blue and asked if he would), Michael Martone (my mentor—I was only able to achieve Andrew Farkas because he is so Michael Martone), and Kathleen Rooney (the true spirit of the Chicago literary scene, whom I was lucky enough to frequently do readings with in the 2010s). I thank all of you for being kind enough to write blurbs.

I am deeply indebted to Louise Krug and Carl Peterson for reading these essays in early drafts. For their efforts, I name them each Honorary Indoorspersons.

I would also like to thank the following people for their assistance: James Tadd Adcox, Kelly Branagan, Steve Byrd, Walter Coronity II, Matt Dickinson, Stefanie Farkas (my sister), Steve Farkas (my dad), Travis Hessman, Whitney Holmes, Phil Jensen, Lauren Loya, Buddy MacKinder, Carol Malivuk (my mom), Lewis Moyse, Patrick Parks, Ashley Walker, Adrianna Ramos, Diana Satruc, John Schloman, Scott Schulman, Jason Teal, the Twentysomethings (Helen, Jasmine, Scoles, Tanner, and Trang), Luis Urrea, Sara Watts, Jim Westlake, Patrick Wilson, Brooke Wonders, and Maria Ortiz, who, like the Lady of the Lake (Michigan), gave me the title of The Great Indoorsman.

CPSIA information can be obtained
at www.ICGtesting.com
Printed in the USA
LVHW010929150222
711104LV00007B/681